EASY
KOSHER
COOKING

EASY KOSHER COOKING

ROSALYN F. MANESSE

JASON ARONSON INC.
Northvale, New Jersey
London

This book was set in 11 pt. Palatino

10 9 8 7 6 5 4 3 2 1

Library of Congress Cataloging-in-Publication Data
Manesse, Rosalyn F.
     Easy kosher cooking / Rosalyn F. Manesse.
        p.   cm.
     Includes index.
     ISBN 1-56821-903-2 (alk. paper)
     1. Cookery, Jewish.   2. Low-fat diet—Recipes.   3. Milk-free diet—
Recipes.   4. Kosher food.   5. Quick and easy cookery.   I. Title.
TX724.M283   1996
641.5'676—dc20   96-5189
                                                                      CIP

Manufactured in the United States of America. Jason Aronson Inc. offers books and cassettes. For information and catalog write to Jason Aronson Inc., 230 Livingston Street, Northvale, New Jersey 07647.

Dedicated to my beloved husband, Ira;
to my children, Marion, Seth, and Ella;
and to my grandchildren, Daniel, Sara, and Jacob.

My son, eat honey, for it is good;
Let its sweet drops be on your palate.
Know: such is wisdom for your soul;
If you attain it, there is a future;
Your hope will not be cut off.
Proverbs 24:13–14
(THE WRITINGS—KETHUBIM
[Jewish Publication Society])

Contents

Spendthrift

Treasure, dollars, casks of jewels,
For a miser, money rules.
Quarters, pennies, nickels, dimes,
Steadily my balance climbs.
I number, total, and I mark it,
Then blow it at the supermarket.

Foreword

There is an old adage that you are what you eat. For the Jew, this statement defines what has been a truism since the revelation at Sinai. More than any other observance, except for Shabbat, the laws of Kashruth have uniquely preserved our identity among the nations, while allowing us to integrate the unique cuisines of the world into our gastronomic repertoire. The goal of *Easy Kosher Cooking* is admirable. How many times have I heard the excuse that it's too hard to cook kosher? How many times have we all dreaded the task of cooking a dinner? The answer is—more than I care to admit. But Rosalyn Manesse has most capably achieved her goal. I have read some of her recipes: they look delicious and I hope to try one of them tonight.

But why another kosher cookbook? In our kitchen, eight kosher cookbooks sit on our counter for ready reference, in addition to the numerous volumes on our bookshelves.

Kosher food has entered the age of health-consciousness and cultured palates. First-class kosher wines successfully compete in international invitational competitions. The connoisseur of kosher food, whether due to observance or intrigue, demands quality cuisine. Be it Eastern European, Mediterranean, American, French, or Nouveau, the dish must be tasty and not defined by the old caricature of drowning in chicken fat. *Easy Kosher Cooking* is the cookbook for this new age of kosher food.

Like most religions and cultures, Judaism has periods of days for feasting and celebrating with food. However, the similarity ends with Kashruth, the laws governing eating in Judaism. Kosher is not a style, nor a cuisine. Kashruth is a way of life. Kosher food is not reserved for an occasion such as a Bar Mitzvah or wedding. Kosher is an all-encompassing word that denotes acceptability for the Jew. We speak of kosher Torah scrolls, and when people say "something isn't kosher," they usually mean something isn't right, that it isn't acceptable. The regulations guiding the kosher lifestyle may seem daunting at first when one is confronted by the magnitude of legislation found in the code of Jewish law. However, it must be remembered that Judaism is a religion whose continuity is based on an oral tradition, that most laws are handed down and learned from parent to child or grandparent to grandchild, much like a child learns how to walk, talk, dress, and eat. Each law was learned by observing others and then practicing what was observed.

Another aspect of kosher living is the mode of eating. Judaism rejects gluttony. A meal is eaten while seated. Food should not be eaten "on the run." The blessings before partaking of food and the grace after a meal prevent the meal from being rushed. The dining table is like an altar in the Jewish household. Food is treated with respect. Meat and poultry are eaten only after they are painstakingly prepared. Each step of this preparation, from *shechita*, ritual slaughter, to *kashering*, soaking and salting, serve to heighten our awareness that we are eating something that was once living and had blood pulsing through its veins. Jews are enjoined from eating meat and dairy together. Although this is a biblical commandment, our Rabbis, of blessed memory, saw in this an important metaphor. We cannot mix death, which is represented by meat, with life, which is represented by milk.

Clearly, diet occupies an important position in Judaism. Kosher cooking sets out to combine religious loyalty with distinctive tastes of the societies in which the Jews found themselves in history. Of course, the laws of Kashruth, which prohibit certain foods and the mixing of other foods, engender a creativity in cooking.

The laws of Kashruth also led to the development of certain dishes that are associated with certain holidays. The classic *cholent*, a stew that is left on a covered fire overnight for the Shabbat, is not unique to the Eastern European Jew. Each Jewish community in the Middle East and Far East has its own type of *cholent*, albeit known by different names. The main difference is the type of beans and seasonings used in each. Even among the Ashkenazi Jews, different seasonings make distinctive *cholent*s based on one's unique heritage.

Israel, being the magnet country for all Jews, and the United States, being a country with open arms for all cultures, have helped Jewish cooking achieve great new heights, as each Jew, from wherever he or she may come, can now share culinary expertise and open up the way for even greater experiments with kosher cooking.

So it is with *Easy Kosher Cooking*. I hope for all the budding kosher cooks, and for the experienced ones as well, *hatzlacha raba*, great success, in all your kosher endeavors.

Rabbi Tszvi Klugerman

Acknowledgments

Thanks to the following for encouragement and advice:

Ira Manesse
Marion and Lawrence Schack
Seth and Charlene Manesse
Ella Manesse
Michael Taylor
Anne Bleeman
Isabel and Jeff Mencher
Rabbi Tszvi Klugerman

Introduction

I hope that these recipes will bring enjoyment to you and your loved ones.

There is an old saying, "It's difficult to be Jewish." Although observing the Jewish laws of Kashruth may not be easy, kosher cooking itself does not have to be complicated. I have written *Easy Kosher Cooking* to prove that point. It is a book for today's cook, who wants quick and easy, low-fat cooking, using minimally processed products. The more than 360 tested recipes call for nourishing, inexpensive ingredients.

This book is full of everyday, favorite family recipes. Although I include holiday recipes, my book is geared toward the daily family cooking and to getting some delicious, nourishing food on the table for a hungry household with the least possible fuss. That is what I mean by the word *Easy* in the title. I include everyone's favorites, like spaghetti, stews, and soups, with easy, home-style preparation.

The recipes are uncomplicated, and there are no fancy sauces. There are many one-dish meals, which can be put on the stove or slipped into the oven, leaving time for other pursuits while the meal cooks.

I realize that people nowadays are warned to decrease the amount of red meat and fats they eat. Therefore, my book offers many non-meat main dishes for the kosher cook: besides fish and poultry chapters, there is an entire chapter consisting of thirty-three vegetarian and dairy main dishes.

Many of the foods are flavored with herbs like parsley, basil, and thyme instead of being heavily salted.

I include everyone's favorite foods—and all the recipes are home tested—including things like pizza, goulash, vegetable soup, chocolate cookies.

For ease of preparation, my recipes are simplified and stream-lined, but the instructions are complete and easy to follow. Most only involve one or two steps. Some recipes are so easy that they can be used to teach children how to cook. For example, there are several no-bake cookie recipes and some appetizers, such as the Pink Mayonnaise Dip, that children will enjoy making and eating.

There are beloved old recipes handed down in the family, such as my Grandma's strudel and my Aunt Lil's pancakes. There are traditional Jewish recipes such as tzimmes, chicken soup, and *cholent*. But there are new and different items also—items that are unusual for a kosher cookbook—like bok choi soup, tomato salsa, tofu chop suey, and Irish soda bread.

I never lose sight of this being a kosher cookbook and so have included lots of ideas for Jewish holiday foods—with two chapters for Passover; suggestions for cakes and cookies for Rosh Hashanah, the New Year of the Trees; ideas for Sukkot; and of course, traditional cookies for Purim. And there is a large chapter following this one on "Jewish Holiday Menu Suggestions." This includes a brief description of each holiday.

Besides these, there are many parve (containing neutral foods, with neither meat or milk) recipes—for vegetables and desserts that contain no milk, so that they can be eaten with meat meals, in accordance with the laws of Kashruth.

Even so, you don't have to be Jewish to use and enjoy this practical cookbook. These foods are family favorites for most people—including meat loaf, chicken baked in barbecue sauce, chocolate cake. There is a handy glossary and Jewish holiday menu suggestions for those unfamiliar with Jewish expressions, foods, or the holidays.

Under the heading of health, many of the recipes in *Easy Kosher Cooking* are helpful to those with allergies to dairy products. This is because I include many cake and cookie recipes that do not call for milk or milk products. My Fancy Applesauce Cake recipe and Ira's Fruit Cake require neither eggs nor milk.

My recipes have easy-to-obtain ingredients. They do not call for anything exotic or anything that cannot be bought at an ordinary store. The herbs are all easily available, such as oregano, curry powder, paprika, and celery salt.

Jewish cooking is international—there are recipes from Israel, France, Italy, Great Britain, Canada, Mexico, the Philippines, and many other countries.

Judaism has many important rules about what foods may be eaten, according to the laws of Kashruth. The purpose of the laws is to enable people to elevate the physical act of eating to a higher level and to bring holiness into everyday life.

"In the beginning, God created the heaven and the earth." The Torah begins with what we call today "the environment," teaching us that the Almighty created sky, earth, and water; and the life that teems throughout all of it.

There, right at the start of the Torah, is the story of Adam and Eve. And that story is concerned with what Adam and Eve ate. For they were permitted to eat all of the fruits except for the fruit of one tree, the Tree of Knowledge. Thus, we learn how important what we eat can be.

The story of Noah teaches us tender concern for the welfare and survival of the animal species. Among the first laws given in the Torah—and it is given to all people, not only Jews—is to be kind to animals. "You must not eat flesh with its life-blood in it" (Genesis 9:4).

In the Book of Exodus 22:30 is the law, "You shall be holy to me: you must not eat flesh torn by beasts in the field." Another important law is Exodus 23:19, "You shall not boil a kid in its mother's milk."

Since the Kashruth laws require delicate sensitivity to cruelty to animals, even though we eat meat we need to carefully slaughter the animals in order to eliminate their suffering. A specially trained man, a *shochet*, who is a ritual slaughterer, kills the kosher animals.

We need to be careful of how our meat is cooked. Throughout centuries, our teachers, rabbis, and sages have taught us how to follow the laws of Kashruth in order to guide us on the path of "You shall be holy."

Food plays an important part in the religious life of the Jewish people today. Each day, when we eat, we thank the Almighty for His creation, which "brings forth bread from the earth."

On each Jewish holiday, except for fast days, food plays a significant role. For example, on Passover, no regular bread, but only unleavened bread, called matzo, may be eaten.

Reform Jews generally do not follow the laws of Kashruth. However, many enjoy making traditional Jewish foods, particularly for the holidays.

KASHRUTH

For complete information about the laws of Kashruth, consult a rabbi. There are several books available that give good information on the subject.

The laws of Kashruth enable people to ennoble their lives by following the Almighty's commandments while nourishing their bodies.

All meats and poultry must be kosher. They must have been slaughtered according to Jewish dietary laws. The meat must be soaked and salted carefully, following the laws of Kashruth. Certain animals, such as pigs, are forbidden.

No milk and meat products may be cooked and/or served together. There must be separate pots and dishes for each.

Kosher fishes have fins and scales. No shellfish is allowed.

All fruits and vegetables are allowed, as long as they have been prepared in a kosher manner.

Food that is neither milk or meat, such as fruits, vegetables, and eggs, is parve (neutral) and may be eaten at any time, with any meal.

Jewish Holiday
Menu Suggestions

THE CALENDAR

Judaism follows an ancient calendar. It is a lunar calendar with months lasting either twenty-nine or thirty days and beginning at each new moon. However, the lunar calendar has only 354 days. Therefore, there are leap years with an added month to adjust the calendar. All this causes the Jewish holidays to appear at different times each year on our regular, secular calendar.

SHABBAT, THE SABBATH

The Sabbath begins at sunset on Friday and ends at sunset on Saturday. It is a day of rest. It is welcomed to the home by lighting candles, and reciting prayers over wine and bread. The Sabbath table is set with a white tablecloth, and the Sabbath is ushered in with prayers, joy, and singing.

It is customary to serve two braided loaves of bread, called challah. They are covered with a white cloth until it is time to say the kiddush (grace). It is traditional to serve kosher wine or grape juice. The kiddush prayer is said over the wine, sanctifying the day.

Salads, like macaroni salad, are good selections to make on Friday. It is customary to cook *cholent* or soup on Friday to serve as a hot meal on Saturday. A fire may not be lighted on the Sabbath, so the food is kept warm until serving. In warm weather, cold chicken or fish are often served on Saturday.

Friday Evening Menu

Wine
Challah
Chicken Soup
Oven Easy Chicken
Green Beans Lyonnaise
L.A. Rice
Cucumber Pickle Salad
Fancy Applesauce Cake or Brownies
Tea

Saturday Meal

Wine
Challah
Simple Salad
Cholent
Fresh fruit
Cookies or cake

ROSH HASHANAH, THE JEWISH NEW YEAR

Rosh Hashanah literally means "Head of the Year." It is the New Year. Rosh Hashanah and Yom Kippur are referred to as the High Holy Days. They are the most holy days of the Jewish Calendar. Rosh Hashanah is celebrated on the first two days of the New Year, and Yom Kippur occurs on the tenth day. These ten days are called the Days of Awe.

On Rosh Hashanah, the shofar is sounded. It is a mitzvah (commandment) to hear the shofar blown on the New Year. The shofar is a wind instrument made from a ram's horn. In ancient times, it was used to warn the people, to call them together, or to remind them of important events.

At the end of the prayer service it is customary for people to wish each other a good New Year. If relatives or friends live at a distance, many people mail greeting cards.

Yom Kippur is the Day of Atonement. It begins at sunset. The beautiful prayer, Kol Nidre, opens the service. This haunting prayer is centuries old.

Yom Kippur is a fast day. Healthy adults refrain from eating or drinking until the sun has set and the Holy Day comes to a close. During this day, the time is devoted to prayer, repentance, and reflection.

For Rosh Hashanah, a round-shaped challah is baked, which symbolizes the coming around of another year. Apples and honey are eaten, to wish everyone a sweet year. Honey cake is the traditional dessert, also intended to wish for a sweet year.

Cooked carrots are often served, as they are coin-shaped, and symbolize prosperity. Fresh fruit is also eaten.

Another custom is to serve fish, which is the symbol of abundance. In many families, the fish head is especially prized.

On the second day of Rosh Hashanah, it is customary to eat a fruit that is either newly ripened at this time of year or one not ordinarily eaten by the family. The prayer thanking the Almighty for enabling us to reach this season can then be recited.

A typical holiday meal would include gefilte fish, turkey or roast, and an abundance of vegetables.

Rosh Hashanah Menu

Wine
Round-shaped Challah
Apple slices with honey
Gefilte Fish Salad
Lentil Vegetable Soup
Roasted Chicken or Turkey
Carrot Tzimmes
Potatoes Blossom
Fresh fruit
Easy Honey Cake or New Year Cookies

SUKKOT, THE HARVEST FESTIVAL

Sukkot is a harvest festival and has been called "The Jewish Thanksgiving." Decorations of fruit, vegetables, and greenery are customary. Jews build a temporary shelter, called a sukkah, outdoors. It is not only a symbol of the harvest season, but also a reminder of how our ancestors lived when they traveled through the desert on their way from Egypt to the Promised Land.

The sukkah must be constructed under the open sky, with no roof or tree overhanging it. Its roof is covered with branches, vines, or grasses. The stars must be visible through this roof. If, however, the weather is bad, the meal is eaten indoors.

During Sukkot, it is a mitzvah (commandment) to recite prayers over the *lulav* and *etrog*, which are branches of the palm tree, willow, and myrtle, plus the citron fruit.

At the end of the eight-day Sukkot holiday, Simchat Torah (the Rejoicing of the Torah) is celebrated. All through the year, portions of the first five books of the Holy Scriptures have been read. On this day, the reading will be completed and begun anew at the beginning. It is celebrated by processions, singing, and dancing.

Fresh fruits and vegetables are served. For convenience in eating outdoors in the sukkah, casseroles, sandwiches, salads, or barbecues are suggested.

Sukkot Menu

Wine or grape juice
Challah
Coleslaw
Arroz Con Pollo or Crock Pot Stew
Fresh Fruit Cake
Beverage
Nuts, fresh fruits

CHANUKAH, THE FESTIVAL OF LIGHTS

Chanukah is the Festival of Lights. It occurs at the darkest time of the winter. It is celebrated by lighting candles each night of the eight-day holiday, using a special candlestick, called a *chanukiah* or menorah. One candle is lit on the first night, and on each succeeding night, an additional candle is lit. Every night, there is also an extra candle lighted, called the *shammash*.

Chanukah commemorates an historic event. In the year 165 B.C.E., the Jewish people were ruled by King Antiochus of Syria. Antiochus wanted all of his kingdom to adopt the Greek civilization, including the Greek religion.

The Jews, led by Judah Maccabee, fought a war for their religious freedom. At last, the Temple in Jerusalem was liberated. Then it had to be purified. After the altar had been renewed, the people wanted to rekindle the Temple light, but they found only one small jar of oil. They lit this oil and, miraculously, it lasted for eight days, until more oil could be prepared.

Besides candle lighting, Chanukah is celebrated by gift giving, singing, and games. A special spinning top called a dreidel is given to children. Family and friends gather together for a festive meal.

Potato pancakes, called latkes, are traditionally served. They are cooked in oil, which brings to mind the story of the holy oil used in rededication of the Temple in Jerusalem.

In Israel, jelly doughnuts are eaten during Chanukah. In many families, cookies in Chanukah shapes are traditional.

Chanukah Menu

Appetizers—chips or sliced fresh vegetables and dip
Los Angeles Salad
Turkey
Rice Stuffing
Broccoli
Potato Latkes and applesauce
Chanukah Cut-Out Cookies
Sponge Cake

TU B'SHEVAT, ARBOR DAY

Tu B'Shevat, the New Year of the Trees, is on the fifteenth day of the Hebrew month of Shevat. This holiday originated in ancient Israel and was the day from which to count the age of a tree.

Tu B'Shevat is the Jewish Arbor Day. In Israel, trees are planted on this day. Those who cannot plant a tree in person often send a donation for one to be planted.

The holiday is observed by eating fruits, especially fruits that grow in Israel. Some of these include grapes, raisins, oranges, figs, dates, carob, grapefruit, apples, and nuts. It is also fun to eat some fruit cookies or cakes.

Tu B'Shevat is a time to appreciate the wonders of our world, especially trees and forests, and to make efforts to plant, conserve, and care for them.

PURIM

Purim is a happy holiday celebrating the salvation of the Jews from Haman, the Persian tyrant. The story of Purim is found in the biblical Book of Esther (the Megillah), which is read in the synagogue on this holiday.

The story tells how the brave queen of Persia, Esther, saved her people from the persecution of the prime minister, Haman.

Purim is celebrated with masquerades and parties. A big family dinner is traditional.

Cookies, called *Hamantaschen* (Haman's Hat) are eaten on Purim. It is customary to exchange gifts of sweets and fruits, and to wear costumes. Gifts of food to the poor are also given.

Purim Menu

Appetizers—Chopped Liver, sliced vegetables
Rye bread or pita bread with Hummus
Honey Roasted Chicken or Brisket of Beef
Roast Vegetables
Waldorf Salad
Prune *Hamantaschen*
Tea

PESACH, PASSOVER

Before Passover, the house is thoroughly cleaned and bread crumbs are collected and burned in a ceremony to symbolically remove all leaven from the home. This ceremony reminds people to cleanse their lives and minds and to make a new start. On Passover, different dishes, pots, and cutlery are used.

Passover, an eight-day-long holiday, is a reminder of the Exodus from Egyptian slavery. During this time, no regular bread or cake is eaten, but only unleavened bread called matzo and special, kosher-for-Passover cake.

Passover is celebrated in the home, by a special ceremony and meal, called the seder. There is a ceremonial seder plate on the table, on which is placed *a roasted egg, a roasted (lamb) bone, bitter herbs* (usually horseradish), *haroseth or charoses* (usually a mixture of grated apples and ground nuts), *a green vegetable* (parsley or celery tops), and some *romaine lettuce* (also considered a bitter herb). Also placed on the table are three matzos, which are piled one on top of the other. They are covered with a cloth. They symbolize the three types of Jews—Cohens (priests), Levites, and Israel.

A special wine cup is placed on the table for Elijah the Prophet, who is symbolically invited to each seder meal. A bowl of salt water recalls the tears shed by the slaves in Egypt. Parsley is dipped in the salt water.

"Let all who are hungry, come and eat" is recited on Passover; and indeed, large meals of chicken soup, matzo, and many delicacies are served. But before Passover, it is customary to donate money to enable those who do not have the means to still celebrate Passover. It is often the custom for families to invite "strangers," such as students away from home or newcomers, to their homes for the seder.

Passover Menu

Seder Plate Foods
Matzo
Boiled eggs with salt water
Chicken Soup and Matzo Balls
Turkey
Apple Kugel
Orange Yams
Cucumber Salad
Cranberry Sauce, pickles
Pickled Peppers
Passover Sponge Cake, Macaroons
Tea

LAG B'OMER

We count the fifty days of the Omer from Passover to Shavuoth. Lag B'Omer is the thirty-third day. This was the time of the barley harvest in ancient Israel. Tradition teaches that on this day, a severe plague among young scholars ceased.

Lag B'Omer is celebrated by having picnics and archery games.

Lag B'Omer Menu

Hot Dogs or sandwiches
California Pasta Salad
Potato Salad
Fresh Fruit
Cookies

SHAVUOTH, PENTECOST

Shavuoth it is the anniversary of the giving of the Ten Commandments at Mount Sinai. Shavuoth is also an agricultural festival. It is the time of the harvest of the Firstfruits.

One of the ways of observing the holiday is to study the biblical Book of Ruth. In many synagogues, teenage children have confirmation ceremonies.

The home is decorated with flowers or greenery. On Shavuoth, fish and dairy foods, such as kugels, and milk soups, are served.

Shavuoth Menu

Wine
Challah
Isabel's Famous Dip, with sliced raw vegetables
Baked Salmon
Pickled Vegetables
Aunt Evelyn's Noodle Pudding
Ira's Fruit Cake
Fresh fruits

For Reference

c	cup
lb	pound
oz	ounce
pkg	package
qt	quart
T	tablespoon
tsp	teaspoon

COOKING TERMS

Baste   To moisten food during the cooking process by spooning liquid over it as it cooks.

Batter   A thin mixture.

Crouton   A small cube of toast.

Dice   To cut into small cubes.

Fold   To gently add to a mixture, usually with a spatula.

Garnish   To trim with small pieces of food, such as parsley or lemon slices.

Lyonnaise   Cooked with onions.

Saute   To cook in a small amount of fat.

Score   To make some shallow cuts on the surface of the food.

Simmer   To cook in liquid, over low heat, so that bubbles form at a slow rate.

WEIGHTS AND MEASURES

dash	less than 1/4 teaspoon
3 teaspoons	1 tablespoon
16 tablespoons	1 cup
1 cup	8 fluid ounces
2 cups	1 pint
4 cups	1 quart
4 quarts	1 gallon
1.06 quarts	1 liter
1 cup	237 milliliter
1 tablespoon	15 milliliter
1 quart	946 milliliter

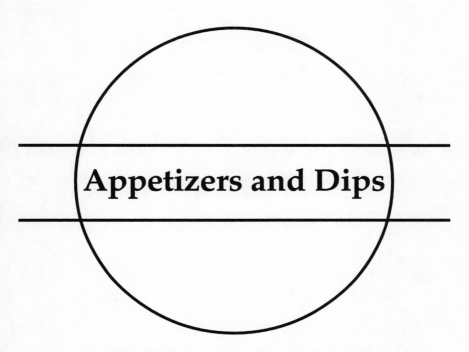

Appetizers and Dips

Ever since Abraham and Sarah welcomed the three angels to their home (Genesis 18:1–17), hospitality has been one of the important principles of Judaism.

CHEESE CANAPÉS (MILK)

Your kids can help to make this easy recipe for a party.

crackers or melba toast
cream cheese, plain or flavored—such as pimiento cream cheese
sliced olives (optional)

Spread cream cheese on the crackers and serve on a tray, garnished with olives.

CHOPPED LIVER (MEAT)

This is the famous Jewish dish. In order to be kosher, liver must be prepared according to the dietary laws. This recipe is suitable for Passover.

½ lb liver, or 5 chicken livers
1 slice onion
2 hard-cooked eggs
2 T mayonnaise or rendered chicken fat (schmaltz)
salt and pepper

Wash the liver, score it with a knife, salt it, and broil it so that blood drips off. Wash it again, and chop with the onion and eggs. Add remaining ingredients. Serve with crackers, matzo, or rye bread.

COCKTAIL FRANKS (MEAT)

This is something quick to serve to a hungry crowd. Teenagers love them.

**package of cocktail franks (miniature hot dogs) or regular hot
    dogs, cut in 1 inch slices**
ketchup
mustard

Simmer the franks for 5 minutes. Drain and serve on a plate with toothpicks for spearing them. Pass little dishes of mustard and ketchup for dipping.

CUCUMBER COCKTAIL (PARVE)

This easy recipe uses purchased chili sauce—usually found next to the ketchup in the store. It is made ahead of time, so you can enjoy your guests instead of fussing around in the kitchen.

1–2 cucumbers
½ c chili sauce
2 T lemon juice
1 tsp Worcestershire sauce
1 tsp prepared horseradish
dash of hot pepper sauce
lettuce (optional)

Peel and dice the cucumbers. Mix all ingredients except the lettuce and chill. Serve on lettuce leaves, or in little dishes. Serves four to six.

Variation: One cup flaked cooked fish, like cod, can be substituted for the cucumber.

DEVILED EGGS (PARVE)

Everybody's favorite, even when we are warned about cholesterol. Keep chilled when not being served.

hard-cooked eggs, cooled
mayonnaise or Thousand Island dressing
garnish such as celery, parsley, or paprika (optional)

Remove egg shells and cut hard-cooked eggs in half, lengthwise. Remove the yolks and mash with the mayonnaise or Thousand Island dressing. Replace the yolk inside the eggs. Garnish if desired. Chill.

GEFILTE FISH SALAD (FISH)

A nice way to "doctor" bottled gefilte fish. The same salad can be arranged on individual plates instead. This salad can be served on Passover, too. If olives are not available on Passover, substitute some parsley leaves, radish roses, or celery hearts.

1 jar (24 oz) gefilte fish
4 carrots, sliced
lettuce
1 cucumber, sliced
3 tomatoes, cut up
black olives
1 lemon, sliced thinly

Steam the carrots or cook in water, until tender. Chill. Place lettuce on a platter, and arrange the cucumbers and other ingredients attractively, garnishing with the olives and lemon. Serves six.

GEFILTE TUNA (FISH)

Not a last-minute recipe, as the fish must be refrigerated before cooking.

    1 can (12 oz) tuna, drained
    1 whole egg plus 2 egg whites, beaten
    ½ tsp salt
    dash of pepper
    1 T grated onion
    6 T matzo meal
    6 c water
    another tsp salt
    1 carrot, sliced
    1 small onion, sliced
    1 sprig parsley, or 1 tsp parsley flakes

Mash tuna and mix with eggs, ½ teaspoon salt, grated onion, matzo meal, and pepper. Refrigerate for ½ hour or more. Bring the water and 1 teaspoon salt to a boil. Add the carrot, sliced onion, and parsley. Form the fish mixture into small balls, and drop carefully into the pot of boiling water. Cover tightly, turn heat to simmer, and cook for 45 minutes, without peeking.

GUACAMOLE DIP (PARVE)

This recipe is a great favorite in California and parts west. The lemon juice keeps the avocado from changing color.

    1 ripe avocado
    ½ small onion, grated
    1 T lemon juice
    1 tsp salt
    1 tomato, diced
    few drops of hot pepper sauce

Mash the avocado with the lemon juice. Mix in other ingredients. Serve with raw sliced vegetables or corn chips. Also good as a topping on salads or Mexican-style food.

HUMMUS DIP (PARVE)

This is a well-known Israeli appetizer. Make ahead of time and chill. Serve with sliced vegetables such as celery, carrots, and cucumbers or with cut-up pita bread.

> **1 can (15 oz) garbanzo beans (chickpeas) drained or 2 c home-cooked chickpeas**
> **3 T sesame seeds**
> **4 T water**
> **2 T lemon juice**
> **3 T oil**
> **1 garlic clove, minced**
> **½ tsp salt (optional)**

Process all ingredients except beans in a blender or food processor. Add beans and process until beans are mashed up. You may have to turn off the blender and scrape the sides of the container to grind all the beans. Chill.

ISABEL'S FAMOUS DIP (MILK)

Serve with cut-up vegetables such as celery, carrots, radishes, cauliflower, turnip, and cucumber. Diet mayonnaise and low-fat sour cream may be used. This dip can also double as a salad dressing.

> **½ c mayonnaise**
> **¾ c sour cream**
> **1 T grated onion**
> **1 T chopped fresh parsley or use 1 tsp dried parsley flakes**
> **1 tsp dill weed**
> **1 tsp celery salt**

Mix all ingredients well, and chill.

MARINATED VEGETABLES (PARVE)

This is the way they serve leftover vegetables in France.

Any of the following vegetables, cooked or canned:
green beans
carrots
peas
corn
beets
and
Italian or French dressing
lettuce

Drain the cooked or canned vegetables. Mix with the dressing and chill. Drain and serve on lettuce.

MOCK CHOPPED HERRING (FISH)

This recipe may be made in a food processor. My mother used to make this when I was a little girl. Since she didn't have a food processor then, it was my job to chop it up in a wooden bowl.

1 can (4 oz) sardines, drained and mashed
1 small onion, grated
½ apple, peeled and grated
1 T vinegar (white or cider)
½ tsp sugar
1 hard-cooked egg, chopped
salt and pepper to taste

Mix well and chill. Serve with crackers or small slices of rye bread.

MOCK SOUR CREAM (MILK)

2 T nonfat milk
1 T lemon juice
1 c low-fat or nonfat cottage cheese

Place ingredients in a blender, and blend until smooth. Can be used as a dip for sliced vegetables or a topping for baked potatoes. Makes a good dessert served on top of sliced bananas or strawberries.

NACHOS (MILK)

No exact measurements are give here, as this recipe may be increased or decreased as required. One large baking dish of chips, topped by 1 recipe for Frijoles and 4 slices of cheese will serve approximately three. Serve with salsa on the side.

1 large bag tortilla or corn chips
4 cheese slices or shredded cheese (American, cheddar, or
**   Monterey Jack)**
hot pickled peppers

Top chips with the cheese and bake at 350° for 15 minutes, or heat in the microwave. Serve with the pickled peppers.

NACHOS SUPREME (MILK)

1 large bag tortilla corn chips
canned vegetarian chili beans or 1 recipe Frijoles, heated
4 cheese slices
sliced ripe olives
hot pickled peppers
½ to 1 c sour cream or 1 recipe Mock Sour Cream
½ to 1 c avocado dip or 1 recipe Guacamole (optional)

Top chips with the beans and cheese. Bake at 350° for 15 minutes, or heat in a microwave. Serve topped with the sour cream, olives, peppers, and Guacamole.

NOT CHOPPED LIVER (PARVE)

2 large onions, chopped
1 T margarine or oil
1 can (15 oz) green beans, drained
1 small can (8½ oz) peas, drained
6 hard-cooked eggs
2 c walnuts
salt and pepper

Heat margarine or oil in skillet, and cook onions until limp. Chop all ingredients, or process all ingredients in a food processor. Chill.

PINK MAYONNAISE DIP (PARVE)

What is this pink stuff?

1 c mayonnaise
½ c ketchup
1 T lemon juice

Mix all ingredients. Serve with sliced vegetables such as celery, carrots, radishes, raw cauliflower, cherry tomatoes, cucumber, or bell peppers.
   Variation: Substitute chili sauce for the ketchup.

PORCUPINE

This may be changed from a dairy to a parve dish by omitting the cheese, or to a meat one by substituting chunks of salami or bologna for the cheese. I'll bet you can think of lots of other foods to serve with toothpicks!

toothpicks
½ grapefruit or red cabbage
cubes of cheese
olives

pickled cocktail onions
gherkins
pineapple chunks

Place ½ grapefruit or red cabbage, cut-side down, on a plate. Stick toothpicks in tidbits such as cheese squares, olives, and so forth. Push toothpicks all around into the grapefruit.

RATATOUILLE (PARVE)

A wonderful dish for that bountiful summer harvest. If you have some tomatoes in your garden, substitute 2 cups diced tomatoes for the canned ones.

2 T oil
1 large onion, sliced
2 cloves garlic, minced
1 small eggplant, diced
2 small zucchini, diced
1 green pepper, diced
1 can (16 oz) tomatoes, sliced, including liquid
½ tsp basil
½ tsp oregano
salt and pepper to taste
½ tsp sugar
2 mushrooms, sliced (optional)

Heat oil, add onion and garlic, and cook over medium heat, stirring, for 5 minutes. Stir in eggplant and zucchini and cook 5 more minutes. Add remaining ingredients and heat to boiling. Lower heat and simmer, covered, 45 minutes. Uncover and cook 15 minutes longer. Serve hot or cold. Serves four to six.

SALMON BALL (MILK)

This recipe makes two salmon balls (one can be frozen for later use). Serve with crackers. My sister Isabel gave me this recipe. If possible, use the red horseradish for color.

    1 can (15 oz) salmon, drained and mashed
    8 oz pkg cream cheese
    1 T lemon juice
    2 T grated onion
    1 T prepared horseradish (red)
    1 tsp liquid smoke
    dash of salt
    ½ c chopped walnuts

Mix ingredients, except walnuts, together well. Make into two balls, and roll in the nuts. Chill.

SALSA (PARVE)

Serve as a dip for corn chips, or use as a relish for fish, chicken, or meat. My brother-in-law Jeff uses it for a nonfat salad dressing. For a hotter salsa, add 2 or 3 chopped jalapeno peppers.

    1 small onion or 3 green onions
    1 small bell pepper
    3 medium tomatoes or 4 c cherry tomatoes
    1 rib celery (optional)
    ½ tsp celery salt
    1½ tsp wine vinegar (or to taste)
    3 to 5 drops of tabasco or hot pepper sauce (or more, to taste)

Grind onion, pepper, celery, and tomatoes in food processor, or chop fine. Mix all ingredients. Chill.

STUFFED CELERY (MILK)

This may be changed to a parve appetizer by omitting the cream cheese and cottage cheese, and using egg salad or another nondairy filling.

celery, cut in 2 or 3 inch pieces
cream cheese
olive slices
tuna salad
guacamole
egg salad
cottage cheese

Fill the celery slices with your choice of filling: cream cheese, tuna salad, guacamole, cottage cheese, or egg salad. Garnish with olive slices.

THREE-DAY PICKLES (PARVE)

For this recipe, you need two fat, wide-mouthed, pint-sized jars, which must be thoroughly cleaned. Pickling cucumbers may be used whole instead of the cut-up, regular cucumbers. The easy part about this recipe is that no cooking is required. But the cucumbers must be refrigerated after they are ready. Once chilled, they will keep for about a month.

The reason for using distilled water is to avoid the minerals in regular water, which may cloud the pickle juice.

3–4 cucumbers
1 bay leaf
4 cloves garlic
2 tsp dill seed
2 T vinegar (white)
6 T kosher or noniodized salt
1 dried red chili or 4 tsp pickling spices
bottled distilled water

Cut up the cucumbers into icicles, by slicing each into four long quarters. Then cut the quarters in half in the middle. Carefully stand the cucumbers in the jars. Into each jar put a piece of the bay leaf, 2 cloves of garlic, and 1 teaspoon of the dill seed. If you like hot pickles, add a piece of red chili pepper, or if you like regular pickles, add 2 teaspoon pickling spices to each jar instead. Mix the salt and vinegar with 2 cups of water, and stir well. Pour over the cucumbers, dividing evenly between the two jars. Add more water, if necessary, to cover the cucumbers. Put something in the jar on top of the cucumbers to hold them under the brine. A tiny piece of plastic works fine. Cover the jars and leave in the sun, on a patio, window sill, or kitchen counter, for about 3 days (or longer, depending on the heat of the weather), adding more water if necessary. The pickles will ferment. They will be ready when they start to turn that green, "pickle" color.

WINTER SALSA (PARVE)

This is a tasty relish, and may be served in a nice glass bowl, to accompany fish, meat, or chicken.

1 large can (28 oz) whole, peeled tomatoes
1–2 onions
1 can (4 oz) green chilies
1 tsp lemon juice
2 or 3 T fresh cilantro (optional)
salt to taste

Drain tomatoes and chilies. Chop all ingredients, or put though the food processor. Chill.

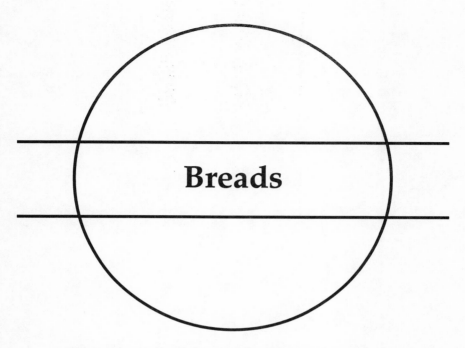

Breads

The secret to making successful yeast bread is to understand that yeast is living fungi. It makes bread rise by fermentation. Therefore, it needs water of a lukewarm or body temperature as well as some sugar to feed upon. The balance of sugar and salt in a recipe is important to regulate the growth of the yeast.

AUNT LIL'S PANCAKES (MILK)

My Aunt Lil and Uncle Maurice are wonderful hosts, and they often have a house full of company. This is our breakfast favorite.

  1½ c all-purpose flour (unsifted)
  2½ tsp baking powder
  ¾ tsp salt
  3 T sugar
  1 egg, well beaten
  1¼ c milk
  3 T melted shortening
  oil

Put all ingredients except oil in a bowl, and stir just enough to moisten (the mixture will be lumpy). Heat some oil in a large skillet, and drop the mixture in by tablespoonfuls. Fry on both sides. Makes 10 to 12 pancakes.

BANANA NUT BREAD (PARVE)

I never met a person who did not like banana bread. (Maybe I don't know enough folks!)

> 3 ripe bananas, mashed
> 2 eggs, beaten
> 2 T oil
> 2 c all-purpose flour
> ¾ c sugar
> 1 tsp salt
> 1 tsp baking soda
> ½ c chopped walnuts

Preheat oven to 350°. Grease a 9 by 5 inch loaf pan. Mix bananas, eggs, and oil. Sift dry ingredients and add, along with nuts. Stir until blended—do not overmix. Spread in the pan and bake for 1 hour, or until done. Place on a cake rack to cool for 10 minutes, then turn out and allow to cool further.

BANANA NUT MUFFINS (MILK)

These are nice for lunches and for snacks.

> 1½ c all-purpose flour (unsifted)
> ⅓ c sugar
> 2 tsp baking powder
> ½ tsp salt
> 2 medium bananas, mashed
> 1 egg, slightly beaten (or egg substitute)
> ½ c milk
> ¼ c oil
> ½ c chopped walnuts
> nonstick spray (optional)

Preheat oven to 400°. Grease muffin tins, or spray with nonstick spray. Combine dry ingredients. Mix banana with egg, milk, and oil. Then mix together with dry ingredients and nuts. Stir until moistened—do not overmix. Fill greased muffin tins ⅔ full and bake for 25 minutes, or until done. Makes 12 muffins.

BATTER BREAD (PARVE)

The secret to making yeast bread is to be careful with the temperature of the added liquid. If it is too hot, it will kill the yeast—which
is a living (although microscopic) organism. If the liquid is too cold,
it will not foster the growth of the yeast. Be sure that the liquid is
about body temperature, by testing a drop on your arm before use.

If you are using bottled yeast, remove the yeast from the refrigerator and allow it to come to room temperature before use.

6 c whole wheat flour (unsifted)
6 c white all-purpose flour (unsifted)
2 T salt
2 pkg dry yeast
½ c molasses
7 c hot tap water

Mix together, in a large bowl, the flours, salt, and yeast. Add the
molasses and water, and stir vigorously about 75 times. The mixture will be soft. Spoon into 4 greased 9 by 5 inch bread pans, cover
with waxed paper, and let set in a warm place until double in size
(about 45 minutes). Preheat oven to 400° and bake 15 minutes. Lower
heat to 350° and cook 50 minutes longer, or until done. Turn out on
cake racks to cool.

BISCUITS (PARVE)

I love this recipe as it is so quick to make. Most biscuit recipes require the cutting-in of shortening, but not this one—oil is used
instead. Plus, by using water for the liquid, the biscuits are parve.
They are nice when served warm, and can be reheated in an oven
or a toaster oven the next day. Biscuits may be served English style,
with tea, or American style, with chicken. Serve with margarine,
butter, honey, jam, soup, or with gravy from stew.

2 c sifted all-purpose flour
1 T baking powder
½ tsp salt
¼ c oil
⅔ c water

Preheat oven to 475°. Set out a cookie sheet and a piece of waxed paper. Mix together the dry ingredients. Add oil and water all at once, and stir quickly until dough sticks together. Knead lightly 6 to 10 times. Turn out dough on the waxed paper, and pat down to about ½ inch thick. (Flour your hand a little bit, to keep dough from sticking.) Cut with floured biscuit cutter or use a knife to cut into 2 to 3 inch squares. Put on the ungreased cookie sheet and bake about 15 minutes, until they are golden and the biscuit bottoms look browned. Serve warm. Makes about 18 two-inch biscuits.

Variation: Instead of water in this recipe, use an equal amount of milk, either regular or nonfat.

BLUEBERRY MUFFINS (MILK)

Everyone's favorite muffin is easier to make with this recipe.

2 c all-purpose flour (unsifted)
3 tsp baking powder
½ tsp salt
3 T sugar
¾ c fresh or thawed frozen blueberries
1 egg, beaten
1 c milk
3 T oil

Line muffin pans with paper or aluminum liners. Preheat oven to 425°. Place dry ingredients in a large bowl and mix. Add the blueberries. Then add the remaining ingredients and mix only until everything blends. Do not beat. Fill the muffin pans about ⅔ full and bake 20 to 25 minutes. Makes 12 muffins.

CORN BREAD (MILK)

This recipe may also be used to make corn muffins. Just put the batter into a greased muffin tin. Makes about 12 muffins. The sugar may be decreased to 2 or 3 tablespoons if a less-sweet muffin is desired. Bake muffins for 20 to 25 minutes, or until done.

1 c corn meal
1 c all-purpose flour (unsifted)
¼ c sugar
1 T baking powder
1 tsp salt
⅓ c oil
1 egg, beaten (or egg substitute)
1 c nonfat milk

Preheat oven to 425°. Grease, or spray with a nonstick spray, an 8 inch square pan. Mix corn meal, flour, sugar, baking powder, and salt in a bowl. Add other ingredients, and mix only until blended. Pour into pan and bake 25 minutes, or until done. Cut into squares.

Variation: For a lighter version of this corn bread, reduce the sugar to 1 tablespoon and the oil to 2 tablespoons. The salt may be omitted, if desired. You may also substitute 2 egg whites for the whole egg.

FRENCH TOAST (MILK)

If unexpected guests stay overnight and you are out of bagels, make French toast for a breakfast treat. Double or triple the recipe, if need be. Serve with the cinnamon-sugar mixture listed here, or with syrup, honey, jam, or confectioners' sugar.

1 egg, beaten (or egg substitute)
1 tsp sugar
⅓ c milk
3 slices bread
2–4 T margarine
cinnamon-sugar mixture (1 tsp cinnamon and ⅓ c sugar)

Mix egg, 1 teaspoon sugar, and milk in a flat bowl. Heat margarine in a frying pan. Dip the bread into the egg mixture, turning to coat both sides. Fry in the margarine until browned on each side. Serve with cinnamon-sugar mixture. Serves two or three.

HONEY QUICK BREAD (MILK)

This bread contains buttermilk. One or two tablespoonfuls of candied fruit peels may also be added, for serving on Rosh Hashanah, Tu B'Shevat, Sukkot, or Shavuoth. Because it has honey in it, it will keep fresh longer than other breads.

2½ c sifted all-purpose flour
1 tsp salt
1 tsp baking soda
2 T shortening
1 c honey
1 egg
¾ c buttermilk
½ c raisins
½ c chopped nuts
nonstick spray (optional)

Preheat oven to 300°. Grease a 9 by 5 by 3 inch loaf pan, or spray with nonstick spray. Sift flour, salt, and soda together. Beat the shortening and honey together, and mix in the egg. Add dry ingredients alternately with the buttermilk. Stir in the raisins and nuts. Bake 1 hour and 30 to 40 minutes.

IRISH SODA BREAD (MILK)

Excellent served warm, with preserves or honey. Contains no eggs.

2½ c all-purpose flour (unsifted)
½ c sugar
½ c raisins (optional)
1½ tsp baking soda
1 tsp salt
1½ c nonfat (skim) milk
1½ T vinegar
1 T oil

Preheat oven to 350°. Grease an 8 inch round cake pan. Mix dry ingredients together. Add remaining ingredients and mix just until blended. Spread in the greased pan. Bake 50 minutes, or until browned and a toothpick inserted in the center comes out clean. Cool on a cake rack.

LEMON POPPY SEED MUFFINS (MILK)

These muffins are very nice when served warm. They require no eggs.

   1½ c sifted all-purpose flour
   ¾ c sugar
   2 tsp baking powder
   1 tsp baking soda
   ¼ tsp salt
   1 T poppy seeds
   ⅔ c plain yogurt
   ⅔ c milk (may be nonfat)
   2 T lemon juice

Preheat oven to 400°. Line muffin pans with paper baking cups. Mix dry ingredients in a large bowl. Add yogurt, milk, and lemon juice. Mix only until dry ingredients are moistened. Bake for 18 minutes, or until done. Remove from pan and cool on rack. Makes 12.

OATMEAL RAISIN MUFFINS (MILK)

These muffins make a nice breakfast treat.

   1 c all-purpose flour (unsifted)
   1 c quick-cooking oatmeal (uncooked)
   3 tsp baking powder
   ½ tsp salt
   2 T sugar
   ½ tsp cinnamon
   ¼ c raisins
   1 egg, beaten (or egg substitute)
   1 c milk (regular or nonfat)
   3 T oil

Preheat oven to 425°. Grease muffin pans. Mix dry ingredients and raisins. Mix together the egg, milk, and oil. Combine ingredients and mix until moistened—do not overmix. Fill muffin pans ⅔ full. Bake for 20 to 25 minutes, or until done, and cool on rack. Makes 12.

PRUNE MUFFINS (MILK)

This recipe may be made into date or raisin muffins instead.

    2 c all-purpose flour (unsifted)
    3 tsp baking powder
    ½ tsp salt
    3 T brown sugar
    1 tsp cinnamon
    1 egg, beaten (or substitute)
    1 c milk (regular or nonfat)
    3 T oil
    ¼ cup prunes, dates (cut up), or raisins
    ¼ c chopped nuts (optional)

Preheat oven to 425°. Grease muffin pans or use aluminum muffin pan liners. Mix dry ingredients, prunes, and nuts. Mix together the egg, milk, and oil. Combine ingredients and mix until moistened— do not overmix. Fill muffin pans ⅔ full. Bake for 20 to 25 minutes and cool on rack. Makes 12.

WHOLE WHEAT MUFFINS (MILK)

Simple to make, and with the wholesomeness of whole wheat.

    2 c whole wheat flour (unsifted)
    3 tsp baking powder
    ¼ tsp salt
    1 T honey
    1 T molasses
    1 egg, beaten
    1 c nonfat milk
    3 T oil

½ c raisins (optional)
nonstick spray (optional)

Preheat oven to 400°. Grease muffin pans, or spray with nonstick spray. Combine dry ingredients and raisins, if used. Mix honey and molasses with egg, milk, and oil. Mix together with dry ingredients. Stir until moistened—do not overmix. Fill greased muffin tins ⅔ full and bake for 25 minutes, or until done. Makes 12.

YEAST BREAD (PARVE)

A challah is a braided bread. It is usually made by braiding 3 long thin ropes, or coils, of dough together. It is customary to serve two challahs on Friday evening, for the Sabbath meal.

This recipe can be used to make regular bread or formed into challah or rolls. For New Year, form the dough into two coils, and twist into a circle; place each in a round cake pan.

Remember that yeast is a living thing. It requires a constant, warm temperature to grow, plus moisture and food. Test the water used in the recipe on your arm, like you would a baby bottle. If yeast is stored in refrigerator, allow to come to room temperature before use.

1 pkg dry yeast
½ c lukewarm water
2 T oil
2 T sugar
1 T salt
2 c lukewarm water
5–6 cups all-purpose flour (unsifted) (2–3 cups of whole wheat
    flour can be substituted for an equal part of the white)
1 egg, separated
1 tsp poppy seeds (optional)

Soak yeast in the ½ cup water for 5 minutes. Place 4 cups of flour in a big bowl, and make a hole in the center. Put in the yeast, oil, sugar, and salt. Add the white of the egg. Gradually stir or beat in the 2 cups of lukewarm water. Mix in the last of the flour by hand, kneading the dough and adding more flour if necessary. Knead about 5 minutes, until the dough is no longer gooey. Put a little oil (about 2 teaspoons) in the bottom of the bowl. Turn the dough in it, to coat the surface. This prevents a hard crust from forming on your dough. Cover with plastic wrap and put a clean dish towel over that.

Now, place in a warm place to rise. If you have an unheated gas oven with a pilot light, that is ideal. Let the dough rise about 1 hour or more, until doubled in size. Punch down, form into loaves, and place in two greased bread pans, covering again as before. Again let rise until double. Mix the yolk with 1 tablespoon water, and brush on top of bread. (This step may be omitted, if you wish). Sprinkle with poppy seeds if desired. Bake at 400° for approximately 40 minutes, until nicely browned. Turn out bread to cool on cake rack.

Famous Four Challah (Parve)

You can make four challahs with this recipe or you can make rolls. Two very large challahs are sometimes served at special events, when a crowd will be attending. Shape in rounds and add raisins for Rosh Hashanah. See Yeast Bread for an explanation of the word *challah*.

> **2 pkg yeast**
> **½ c warm water**
> **¼ c honey**
> **1 T salt**
> **½ c oil**
> **2 eggs, divided, saving 1 yolk for topping**
> **4 c water**
> **12 c (about 5 lb) all-purpose flour (unsifted)**
> **1 tsp poppy or sesame seeds**

Follow method for Yeast Bread, substituting ingredients and forming braids of three coils for each challah. Let challah rise on cookie sheets. This recipe can be used to make 3 challah and 3 pans of rolls. Do not preheat oven. Place bread in the oven and set it at 375°. Bake about 40 to 45 minutes for challah, a shorter time for rolls.

To make two very large challahs, use a preheated oven set at 375° for 45 minutes.

Oatmeal Yeast Bread (Parve)

Try this tasty bread. It makes a nice change from white bread.

1½ c boiling water
1 c uncooked oatmeal
⅓ c shortening
2 pkg dry yeast
½ c lukewarm water
½ c molasses
2 eggs, beaten
1 T salt
3 c whole wheat flour (unsifted)
3¼ c all-purpose flour (unsifted)
2 tsp oil

Place oatmeal and shortening in a large bowl and pour the boiling water over it. Allow to cool for about ½ hour or more. In a small bowl, add the ½ cup lukewarm water to the yeast. Mix together the oatmeal, molasses, eggs, and salt. Add the yeast and whole wheat flour and mix well. Stir in the white flour, kneading until the dough is smooth and elastic. Place in a bowl to which about 2 tsp oil has been added, and turn dough to grease it on all sides. Cover with plastic wrap and a dish towel. Let rise in a warm place until double (about 1 hour). Punch down and form into bread or rolls. Raisins may be added. Cover and let rise. Bake in a 350° oven about 45 minutes for bread or 20 minutes for rolls. Makes 2 loaves or 1 loaf and 1 pan of rolls.

Rolls and Onion Rolls (Parve)

Prepare Yeast Bread recipe. For onion rolls, you will need ½ cup finely chopped onion. After the dough has risen, form into twists, miniature challahs, or round, flat rolls.

To make onion rolls, form dough into flat, round rolls. Place rolls on greased cookie sheets. Cover, and let rise until doubled, about 45 minutes. Brush with egg yolk mixed with 1 tablespoon water. Sprinkle with the chopped onion. Use a small, sharp, pointed knife to dent down the center of each onion roll. Bake at 400° for about 20 minutes, until rolls are browned.

Three Loaf Bread (Parve)

1 pkg dry yeast
½ c warm water
1 egg
½ c shortening
2 c warm water
1 tsp salt
¼ c sugar
1 T wheat germ (optional)
1 T soy flour (optional)
7–8 c all-purpose flour (unsifted)
2 tsp oil

Place the yeast and ½ cup water in a large bowl, and let soften 5 minutes. Add all ingredients except flour and oil. Gradually mix in flour. Knead about 5 minutes. Put oil in a bowl. Place dough in oiled bowl, turning to grease all sides. Cover with plastic wrap and a towel, and let rise in a warm place for about 1 hour, or until doubled. Punch down, shape into three loaves, and let rise in greased pans, covered as before. Place in a cold oven. Turn heat to 400° for 15 minutes. Turn down heat to 375° for 25 more minutes, or until done. Raisins (about ¼ cup) may be added to the bread when shaping into loaves.

ZUCCHINI BREAD (PARVE)

If you like banana bread, you will probably like this tasty variation. If you grow zucchini in your garden, you may *need* this recipe!

3 eggs
1 c oil
1 c sugar
1 c brown sugar, packed
2 tsp maple flavoring
2 c grated zucchini
2½ c all-purpose flour (unsifted)
1 tsp salt

½ c toasted wheat germ
2 tsp baking soda
½ tsp baking powder
1 c chopped walnuts
¼ c sesame seed

Preheat oven to 350°. Grease and flour two 9 by 5 inch loaf pans. Beat eggs, beating in oil, sugars, and maple flavoring. Mix together the flour, salt, wheat germ, baking soda, baking powder, and nuts. Fold in alternately with zucchini. Divide batter into the two pans, and top with the sesame seeds. Bake one hour, or until the breads test done (insert a toothpick in the center—it should come out clean). Cool on racks for 15 minutes. Turn out and cool before slicing.

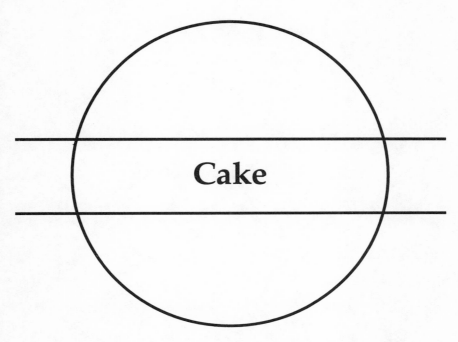

Cake

How do you tell if a cake is done? A cake is done when it springs back when tapped on the top with a finger. An even more "scientific" test is to stick a wooden toothpick in the middle of the cake, if it comes out with dough on it, bake the cake five or ten minutes longer; if the toothpick comes out clean, the cake is done.

APPLESAUCE AND HONEY CAKE (PARVE)

2¼ c sifted all-purpose flour
1 tsp baking soda
½ tsp salt
1 tsp cinnamon
½ tsp allspice
½ c raisins
½ c chopped nuts
½ c shortening
1 c honey
1 egg, well beaten
1 c applesauce

Preheat oven to 350°. Grease a 9 by 9 inch pan with shortening, and line bottom with waxed paper. Sift dry ingredients together, and mix a little flour with raisins and nuts in a separate bowl. Cream the shortening and honey together and beat in egg. Add sifted dry ingredients alternately with the applesauce, and then mix in the raisin mixture. Spread in the pan and bake for 50 minutes, or until cake tests done. Allow to cool in the pan for 10 minutes. Turn out on cake rack, peel off paper, and allow to cool.

CAPE BRETON ISLAND MOLASSES CAKE (PARVE)

Just where is Cape Breton Island? It's part of Nova Scotia.

½ c vegetable shortening
½ c sugar
1 egg
1 c molasses
2½ c sifted all-purpose flour
½ tsp salt
2 tsp baking powder
½ tsp baking soda
1 tsp cinnamon
½ tsp ginger
½ tsp allspice or cloves
¼ c raisins
1 c hot water
nonstick spray

Preheat oven to 350°. Spray a 9 by 9 inch pan with nonstick spray and line with waxed paper. Beat shortening and sugar together. Beat in the egg and molasses. Add all other ingredients, and mix at low speed for two minutes, occasionally scraping the sides of the bowl with a spatula. Turn beater to high, and beat well for 2 minutes. Spread batter in pan and bake for about 40 to 45 minutes, or until cake is done. Cool on a rack for 10 minutes, then turn cake out and peel off paper.

CHOCOLATE CAKE (PARVE)

At last, a chocolate cake that contains no milk! For frosting, see the Seven Minute Icing in the "Passover Desserts," or use the Easy Frosting at the end of this chapter.

1 c shortening
2½ c sugar
1½ tsp vanilla
3 eggs

3 c sifted all-purpose flour
½ tsp salt
1½ tsp baking soda
3 squares unsweetened baking chocolate or 8 T cocoa plus 2 T
    shortening
1½ c cold water

Preheat oven to 350°. Grease two 8 inch square pans or one 9 by 13 inch pan and line with waxed paper. Melt chocolate in a double boiler over hot water. Cream shortening, beating in sugar. Beat in eggs, one at a time. Add vanilla and chocolate. Sift dry ingredients, and add alternately with water. Spread in pan and bake for 30 minutes for layers, and 30 to 45 minutes for a large pan (until cake tests done). Cool in pan on rack for 10 minutes. Turn out on rack, and remove waxed paper. Allow to cool completely before frosting.

COCOA CAKE (PARVE)

Good with chocolate icing.

¾ c shortening, melted
6 T cocoa powder
2 c all-purpose flour
1½ c sugar
1 tsp baking powder
⅛ tsp salt
1 tsp baking soda
2 eggs
1 c water
1 tsp vanilla

Preheat oven to 350°. Melt shortening. Grease and line with wax paper a 9 by 13 inch pan or two 8 inch layer pans. Sift dry ingredients into a large bowl. Add all other ingredients and beat well. Spread in pan and bake for 40 minutes, or until done. Allow to cool in pan on rack for 10 minutes. Invert, peel off wax paper, and cool completely.

COFFEE CAKE (PARVE)

There is no coffee in this cake; rather, it is meant to be served along with coffee.

3 eggs
1¼ c sugar plus approximately 1 T for top of cake
½ c oil
grated rind of half a lemon
juice of 1 lemon
2 c all-purpose flour
¼ tsp salt
3 tsp baking powder
½ c water
1–2 tsp cinnamon
¼ c raisins
¼ cup chopped nuts and/or coconut or candied fruit (optional)

Preheat oven to 350°. Grease a 12 by 8 by 2 inch pan. Beat eggs and add sugar. Beat well. Stir in oil and then beat in lemon rind and juice. Sift together flour, salt, and baking powder, and beat in alternately with the water. Place half the batter in the bottom of the cake pan and cover with the cinnamon, raisins, and other ingredients desired. Cover with remaining batter. Sprinkle the top with 1 tablespoon sugar. Bake for 1 hour, or until cake tests done.

EASY HONEY CAKE (PARVE)

Honey cake is a traditional food on New Year's. Here's to a sweet year!

1½ c sifted all-purpose flour
¼ c sugar
2 tsp baking powder
¼ tsp baking soda
½ tsp salt
½ tsp ginger
½ tsp cinnamon

½ tsp cloves or allspice
1 egg, well beaten
½ c honey
½ c water
4 T oil
¼ c raisins (optional)

Preheat oven to 350°. Grease a 9 by 9 inch pan, and line the bottom with waxed paper. Sift dry ingredients together. Mix together the egg, water, honey, and oil. Combine all ingredients and beat together. Pour into pan and bake for 30 minutes, or until done. Allow to cool in pan for 10 minutes. Turn out on cake rack, peel off paper, and allow to cool.

FANCY APPLESAUCE CAKE (PARVE)

There are no eggs or milk in this spicy cake.

½ c all-vegetable shortening
1 c firmly packed brown sugar
1 c applesauce
2¼ c sifted all-purpose flour
½ tsp baking soda
½ tsp salt
1 tsp baking powder
½ tsp ground cloves
½ tsp cinnamon
¼ tsp nutmeg
⅓ c chopped nuts
⅓ c raisins
⅓ c currants (optional)

Preheat oven to 325°. Grease a 9 by 5 by 3 inch pan, and line the bottom with waxed paper. Mix shortening and sugar, beating well. Add applesauce. Mix nuts, raisins, and currants in with the flour and add to shortening mixture, along with all other ingredients. Mix well. Pour into pan and bake for 1 hour, or until cake tests done (test with a toothpick). Cool on a rack for 10 minutes, then remove from pan and peel off the waxed paper. After the cake is cold, it may be frosted with plain frosting, if desired, and decorated with candied cherries and nuts. This cake may be wrapped well and frozen (unfrosted). It will keep for 4 months in the freezer. Thaw, wrapped, at room temperature.

FRESH FRUIT CAKE (PARVE)

This is not what you would call an elegant cake, but it is a moist dessert.

¼ c melted margarine
1 c all-purpose flour (unsifted)
1 c sugar
½ tsp cinnamon
⅛ tsp salt
½ tsp baking powder
½ tsp baking soda
1 egg
1 tsp vanilla extract
½ c chopped walnuts
2 c chopped apples or peaches
nonstick spray

Melt the margarine. Preheat oven to 375°. Grease an 8 by 8 inch pan, or spray with nonstick spray. Mix dry ingredients, egg, vanilla, and melted margarine. Stir in nuts and fruit. Spread in prepared pan and bake for 30 minutes. Cool on rack in the pan. Cut in squares when cool.

GOOD TIME CAKE (MILK)

It is important to use all-vegetable shortening at room temperature for this recipe. Almond flavoring can be substituted for the vanilla, if desired. These instructions look long, but actually this is a throw-it-all-in-the-bowl-and-beat-it cake.

May be served with ice cream and/or covered with frosting. Happy Birthday!

2 c sifted all-purpose flour
1½ c sugar
3½ tsp baking powder
1 tsp salt
½ c all-vegetable shortening
1 c milk
1½ tsp vanilla
2 large or 3 medium-sized eggs
nonstick spray

Preheat oven to 350°. Spray a 9 by 13 by 2 inch pan with nonstick spray, and cut out a piece of wax paper to fit the bottom of the pan. Place all the ingredients in a large bowl. Beat with an electric mixer on low until ingredients are blended. Set the beater at high speed, and beat well for 3 or 4 minutes. Interrupt the mixing to scrape the sides of the bowl occasionally with a spatula.

Turn the mixture into the prepared pan, and spread it out neatly. Bake for 40 to 45 minutes, or until done. Cool on a rack for about 10 minutes. Turn the cake out on the rack and peel off the paper. Allow to cool before frosting.

IRA'S FRUIT CAKE (PARVE)

There are no eggs or milk in this cake. One-half cup mixed candied fruits can be substituted for an equal part of the raisins.

2 c light brown sugar, packed
2 c hot water
¼ c shortening
2 c raisins
1 tsp baking soda
2 tsp cold water
3 c all-purpose flour
½ tsp nutmeg
2 tsp cinnamon
½ tsp allspice
1 tsp salt
1½ tsp baking powder

Boil together the brown sugar, 2 cups hot water, shortening, and raisins. Let cool. Add 1 teaspoon baking soda dissolved in 2 teaspoon cold water. Sift together the flour and other dry ingredients and mix all ingredients together well. Pour into a greased and floured 9 by 5 by 3 inch loaf pan. Bake in a preheated 350° oven for 1½ hours, or until done. Set pan on rack for 10 minutes, then turn cake out to cool.

LEKACH HONEY CAKE (PARVE)

This is the traditional recipe for Rosh Hashanah cake.

2 eggs
½ c sugar
¼ c coffee
½ c honey
1 T oil
1¾ c sifted all-purpose flour
⅛ tsp salt
¾ tsp baking powder
½ tsp baking soda
½ tsp cinnamon
½ tsp allspice (optional)
½ c chopped walnuts
2 T brandy (optional)

Preheat oven to 325°. Grease a 9 inch square pan, and line with waxed paper. Beat eggs. Beat in sugar. Add coffee, honey, oil, and brandy. Mix well. Sift the dry ingredients, and mix with the nuts. Gradually add dry ingredients to egg mixture. Beat well. Spread in pan, and bake about 45 minutes, or until cake tests done. Cool on rack. After about 10 minutes, turn out cake and remove paper.

MIGHTY CHOCOLATE CHIP GEMS (PARVE)

Some chocolate chips are dairy—check the label. The gems may be frosted, if desired.

2 eggs, separated
¼ c margarine or shortening
½ c sugar
1 tsp vanilla
⅔ c sifted all-purpose flour
¼ tsp salt
⅛ tsp baking soda
6 oz package of chocolate chips

Line 24 gem cupcake pans with paper linings. Preheat oven to 350°. Measure out ingredients. Beat the egg whites until stiff. Cream together the shortening and sugar. Add egg yolks and vanilla. Beat well. Stir in the flour, salt, and baking soda until well blended (mixture will be thick). Using a rubber spatula, fold in egg whites and then fold in the chocolate chips. Spoon into gem pan and bake 15 to 20 minutes. Makes 24.

MOCHA CAKE (PARVE)

This makes a nice birthday cake. Frost with chocolate icing.

2 c sifted all-purpose flour
1 tsp salt
½ c dry cocoa
1¾ c sugar
½ c shortening
2 eggs
1 tsp vanilla
1 c hot coffee
1 tsp baking soda
½ c boiling water

Preheat oven to 375°. Grease two 9 inch round layer pans or one 9 by 13 inch pan. Line bottoms with waxed paper. Sift flour with the salt and cocoa. Cream shortening in a large bowl, gradually adding sugar. Beat in eggs and vanilla. Alternately beat in flour mixture with the coffee. Dissolve the baking soda in the boiling water and add, beating well. Pour batter into pans. Bake layers for 30 to 35 minutes, or the 9 by 13 pan for 35 to 40 minutes, or until cake tests done. Set on racks for 10 minutes to cool. Turn cake out on racks and peel off paper. Let cool thoroughly before frosting.

PINEAPPLE ALMOND CUPCAKES (PARVE)

1 c brown sugar, packed
½ c margarine or shortening (at room temperature)
1 egg
1 tsp vanilla
2 c sifted all-purpose flour
1 tsp baking powder
½ tsp baking soda
¼ tsp salt
1 can (8 oz) crushed pineapple, undrained
½ c chopped unsalted almonds

Preheat oven to 375°. Set out muffin pans, and line with paper or foil liners. Mix together the sugar, margarine, egg, and vanilla. Stir in other ingredients except almonds and mix well. Then mix in the almonds. Fill the muffin cups about ⅔ full. Bake for 20 minutes, or until cupcakes are done. Makes 18 cupcakes.

SOPHIE'S BANANA CAKE (PARVE)

Chocolate icing is nice on this cake.

¼ c shortening
1 c sugar
1 egg
1 c mashed bananas (2 large)
¼ tsp salt
1½ c sifted all-purpose flour
1 tsp baking powder
1 tsp baking soda
1 tsp vanilla

Preheat oven to 375°. Cream shortening and sugar. Beat in egg and vanilla, and add banana. Sift dry ingredients and beat in. Grease an 8 inch square pan and line with wax paper. Spread in batter and bake for 50 minutes (until cake tests done). Cool on rack for 10 minutes. Turn out cake, and peel off wax paper. May be frosted if desired.

SPONGE CAKE (PARVE)

These are the secrets of sponge cake, as passed down in our family: have the eggs at room temperature, and be careful to separately break each egg into a small bowl. If you get the tiniest bit of yolk into the whites, they will not whip up. The bowl and beaters must be perfectly dry.

You can tell when the egg whites are stiff, because they will stand up in "mountains" and if you make a dent in them with your finger, the dent will stay.

5 eggs, separated
1 c sugar
grated rind of half a lemon
2 T lemon juice
1 c sifted cake flour
¼ tsp salt

Preheat oven to 350°. Set out a 10 inch, two-part tube pan. Measure out all ingredients before starting cake. Sift flour with salt. Beat egg whites until stiff, beating in sugar, 1 tablespoon at a time. Beat yolks with lemon juice and rind until thick and light colored. Using a rubber spatula, fold yolks into whites and then gently fold in flour. Pour into pan. Bake 55 minutes to 1 hour. Remove from oven, and invert pan to cool. Cut out of pan with a knife.

SYDELL'S QUICK COFFEE CAKE (MILK)

1½ c sifted all-purpose flour
½ c sugar
2 tsp baking powder
¼ tsp salt
¼ c oil
1 egg, beaten
½ c nonfat milk
¼ c raisins

Prepare top crumbs (see below). Preheat oven to 350°. Grease a 6 by 10 by 2 inch glass oven pan. Mix dry ingredients. Make a "well" in the center of the flour by piling it on the sides of the bowl. Add the oil, egg, and milk. Mix until ingredients are moistened, and stir in raisins. Spread in the pan and cover with the top crumbs. Bake for 30 minutes, or until done.

Top Crumbs:
¼ c sugar
¼ c all-purpose flour (unsifted)
¼ c margarine
1 tsp cinnamon

Mix the top crumb ingredients with a fork until lumpy. Sprinkle on the cake before baking.

EASY FROSTING

4 c (1 lb) powdered or confectioners' sugar
dash of salt (optional)
¼ c juice, milk, coffee, or hot water
1 tsp vanilla
⅓ c margarine at room temperature

Combine all ingredients and beat until smooth. Add another one or two teaspoonfuls of liquid if necessary. This makes enough frosting for a two-layer cake or a 9 by 13 inch cake.

Variation: For chocolate icing, add 3 tablespoons dry cocoa. For fudge frosting, add ½ cup dry cocoa.

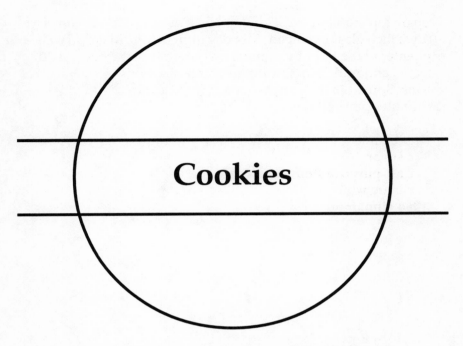

Cookies

One way to avoid overbaking cookies is to use a clock timer to signal when baking time is up. Cool cookies on a wire cake cooler in a single layer.

BROWNIES (PARVE)

Brownies are a popular dessert, and they are quick and easy to make. Bake some if you are expecting a crowd of young people.

²/₃ c sifted all-purpose flour
¹/₃ c cocoa
½ tsp baking powder
½ tsp salt
2 eggs
1 c brown sugar, packed
1 tsp vanilla
¹/₃ c oil
½ c chopped walnuts (optional)

Preheat oven to 350°. Grease an 11 by 7 inch pan. Sift together the flour, cocoa, baking powder, and salt. Beat the eggs and mix in the sugar, vanilla, and oil. Beat well. Gradually stir in remaining ingredients. Spread in the pan and bake for 20 to 25 minutes. Cool in pan on a rack, then cut into bars.

Variation: You may substitute ½ cup white sugar and ½ cup honey for the 1 cup brown sugar.

CANDY COOKIES

These cookies may be dairy if the candies are dairy—check the package.

1 c margarine at room temperature
1 c smooth peanut butter
1 c sugar
1 c firmly packed brown sugar
2 eggs
2 c all-purpose flour (unsifted)
1 tsp baking soda
1½ c candy-coated chocolate candies (¾ lb bag)

Preheat oven to 350°. Mix together the margarine, peanut butter, and brown and white sugars. Beat in eggs, and mix in soda and flour. Mix well, and then fold in the candy. Drop the dough by rounded teaspoonfuls on greased cookie sheets and bake 10 minutes. Watch closely, as the bottoms of these cookies burn easily. Cool on racks. Makes about 4 dozen.

CHANUKAH CUT-OUT COOKIES (PARVE)

The cookie dough must be chilled before rolling out. Keep remaining dough in refrigerator while rolling out part of it.

¾ c margarine at room temperature
1 c light brown sugar, packed
2 eggs
1 tsp vanilla
2¾ c all-purpose flour (unsifted)
1 tsp baking powder
½ tsp salt
nonstick spray
**Topping: ¼ cup white sugar, candy sprinkles, and/or finely
   chopped nuts**

Cream the margarine with the brown sugar. Beat in eggs and vanilla. Mix in the flour, baking powder, and salt. Cover bowl and chill at least two hours (preferably overnight). Preheat oven to 375°. Lightly grease cookie sheets, or spray with nonstick spray. Flour a board and a rolling pin, and roll out part of the dough to between 1/8 and 1/4 inches thick. Cut with cookie cutters or pastry wheel. Place on cookie sheets, and decorate with some sugar or lightly press on sprinkles or nuts. Bake for 7 or 8 minutes, until edges start to brown, and then cool on racks. Then roll out another portion of dough, adding in leftovers from the first batch. Makes about 4 dozen.

CHOCOLATE BARS (PARVE)

¾ c oil
1/3 c cocoa
1 c sugar
2 eggs
1 c all-purpose flour (unsifted)
dash of salt
1 tsp vanilla
1/3 c chopped peanuts
nonstick spray

Preheat oven to 400°. Grease a 9 by 13 by 2 inch pan, or spray with nonstick spray. Mix oil and sugar, and beat in eggs. Stir in remaining ingredients, and beat well. Spread in pan. Bake 15 to 20 minutes, or until a toothpick inserted in the center comes out clean. Cool on rack for 10 minutes, then cut in rectangles.

CHOCOLATE COOKIES (PARVE)

The dough for these cookies must be chilled before baking. This is a plus if you don't have enough time to mix the dough and bake the cookies all at once. This is a delicious cookie.

2/3 c oil
2 c sugar
4 eggs
2 tsp vanilla
2 c sifted all-purpose flour
2 tsp baking powder
½ c cocoa
½ tsp salt
1 c confectioners' sugar

Blend the oil and sugar. Add eggs, beating well after each. Beat in the vanilla. Sift the dry ingredients, except confectioners' sugar. Add to oil mixture and mix well. Cover the dough and chill for 3 hours (up to overnight). Heat oven to 350°. Grease cookie sheets. Drop teaspoonfuls of the dough into the confectioners' sugar, shaping the cookies into little balls. Bake for 10 to 12 minutes. Watch the clock closely, as it is hard to see when the cookies are done. Cool on racks. Makes 6 dozen.

COFFEE SQUARES (PARVE)

Something a bit different from the usual chocolate brownies.

¼ c margarine
1 c brown sugar
1 egg
1 c sifted all-purpose flour
1 tsp baking powder
¼ tsp salt
1 tsp vanilla
¼ c cold coffee
½ c chopped walnuts

Melt margarine in a large pot, and cool. Grease a 9 inch square pan. Preheat oven to 350°. Stir brown sugar into melted margarine. Beat in egg and vanilla. Sift dry ingredients and add alternately with the coffee. Mix in the nuts. Spread in the prepared pan and bake about 30 minutes, or until done. Cool on rack. Cut into squares after cooling about 10 minutes.

ELLA'S CHOCOLATE NO-BAKES (PARVE)

This fun cookie requires no cooking. Children love to make them.

²/₃ c margarine or butter
¾ c sugar
1 T water

3 T cocoa powder
1 tsp vanilla extract
2 c quick-cooking oatmeal (uncooked)
1 c confectioners' sugar

Have margarine at room temperature. Combine with the ¾ cup sugar, water, cocoa, and vanilla and mix well. Then stir in oatmeal. Form into small balls and roll in the confectioners' sugar. Place on a wax paper–lined cookie sheet. Refrigerate until firm. Store in the refrigerator.

GINGER COOKIES (PARVE)

The dough must be chilled, so you can make this dough the day before you make the cookies.

¾ c shortening
1 c sugar
1 egg
¼ c molasses
2 c sifted all-purpose flour
½ tsp salt
2 tsp baking soda
2 tsp ginger
1 tsp cinnamon
¼ tsp cloves or allspice
Topping: ½ c sugar and 2 tsp cinnamon

Cream together the shortening and sugar. Beat in the egg and molasses. Sift together the dry ingredients—except topping—and mix all ingredients together. Cover the dough with plastic and chill several hours. Preheat oven to 350°. Roll teaspoonfuls of dough in the topping mixture and place 2 inches apart on greased cookie sheets. Bake for 12 to 15 minutes, then cool on racks. Makes 3 dozen.

GRANDMA'S STRUDEL (PARVE)

My grandmother called this recipe strudel. She was one of the world's greatest bakers! I remember when she came over to our house to make this recipe for my parents' fifteenth anniversary party and I got to help with all the delicious fillings. This recipe is for a special occasion. I recommend making a paper pattern 8 inches square and using it to cut out the dough layers. Use a sharp knife for cutting out the squares and for cutting the strudel, too.

Fillings:
1 c sugar, mixed with 1 tsp cinnamon
1 c walnuts, finely chopped
⅔ c strawberry jam
¾ c shredded coconut
2 or 3 small cooking apples, sliced thinly
⅓ c raisins or diced dates

Pastry:
4 c sifted all-purpose flour
2 tsp baking powder
½ tsp salt
1 c sugar
½ c oil
2 eggs, beaten
⅓ c water

Make pastry by sifting the flour, baking powder, salt, and sugar into a large bowl. Make a hole in the center, and add the oil, eggs, and part of the ⅓ cup water. Mix, adding the rest of the water gradually, until you have a smooth dough. (Dough will be thick.) Divide the pastry into 5 pieces, one of which is larger than the others. Use a floured board and a rolling pin to roll out the largest piece of pastry to about 13 inches square. Place it in an 8 by 8 by 2 inch square pan, spreading the dough smoothly and extending it up over the sides. If necessary, patch to fit.

Sprinkle part of the sugar and cinnamon mixture over the bottom, along with ½ cup nuts. Roll out the other balls of pastry, and cut to fit the pan. Put one layer in place. Top with part of the jam and half the coconut, then sprinkle with a little of the sugar and cinnamon. Top the next layer with apples and raisins or dates, along with another sprinkle of the sugar mixture. On the next layer, put more jam, nuts, and coconut plus some of the sugar mixture. Put the last piece of pastry on the top, and carefully seal the edges all around. Sprinkle with the remaining sugar and cinnamon. Bake in a preheated 350° oven for 1¼ hours, or until brown. Set pan on rack to cool. Cut in squares to serve.

ISABEL'S CHOCOLATE CHIP BARS (MILK)

These bars are like little candies. There are three ways to make graham cracker crumbs; the first is to buy them ready made, the second is to put graham crackers in between two pieces of waxed paper and roll them with a rolling pin, and the last way is my favorite—crumble the graham crackers slightly as you put them into the food processor. Process until made into coarse crumbs.

   2 c graham cracker crumbs
   6 oz chocolate chips
   1 can (14 oz) sweetened, condensed milk (not the evaporated
      kind)
   1 T honey
   ½ tsp vanilla

Grease a 9 by 9 inch pan. Preheat oven to 350°. Mix together all ingredients and spread in the pan. Bake about 25 minutes. Cool in the pan, on a rack. After cooling for 10 minutes, cut into bars.

JEANETTE'S COOKIES (PARVE)

This is a drop cookie.

   ½ c margarine, at room temperature
   ¾ c sugar
   1 egg
   1½ c all-purpose flour
   ¾ tsp baking soda
   ¼ tsp salt
   ⅓ c molasses
   ½ c chopped unsalted peanuts

Grease cookie sheets and preheat oven to 350°. Cream together the margarine and sugar. Beat in the egg. Sift flour, baking soda, and salt. Add dry ingredients alternately with molasses, mixing well. Stir in peanuts. Drop by teaspoonfuls on cookie sheets, and bake about 12 minutes. Remove to racks to cool. Makes 4 dozen cookies.

NEW YEAR COOKIES (PARVE)

Where I live, Rosh Hashanah can mean hot weather. These honey cookies are only in the oven for 12 minutes and so don't heat the kitchen too much. Moreover, these cookies are a big hit on Chanukah and Purim!

Check carefully—some chocolate chips are dairy.

1½ c sifted all-purpose flour
1 tsp baking powder
1 tsp cinnamon
½ tsp salt
½ c shortening
1 tsp vanilla
¼ c sugar
1 egg
¾ c honey
1 c chocolate chips

Preheat oven to 400°. Grease a 15 by 10 by 1 inch pan. Sift together the flour, baking powder, cinnamon, and salt. Cream together the shortening and sugar. Beat in vanilla and egg. Add honey alternately with the flour mixture. When well mixed, fold in chips. Spread in pan and bake for 12 minutes. Cool on rack and then cut into bars.

NO-BAKE COOKIES (PARVE)

Easy, easy, easy.

¾ c margarine at room temperature
1 c brown sugar, packed
2 c quick-cooking oatmeal (uncooked)

Mix margarine together with sugar and stir in oatmeal. Spread wax paper on a cookie sheet. Drop dough onto wax paper in spoonfuls and refrigerate until firm. Store in refrigerator.

NOVA SCOTIA DATE SQUARES (PARVE)

Yes, I know dates don't grow in Nova Scotia! But this was one of our favorite bar cookies when I lived there. Now I live in California, where the dates *do* grow!

Filling:
2 cups (10–16 oz) chopped dates
¾ c brown sugar
½ c water
1 tsp lemon juice

Cook over low heat for about 15 minutes, stirring. Add a little more water if necessary. Mixture should be thick. Cool.

¾ c margarine at room temperature
½ c firmly packed brown sugar
1 c all-purpose flour (unsifted)
3 c quick-cooking oats (uncooked)
¼ tsp salt
½ tsp baking soda
½ tsp baking powder

Preheat oven to 350°. Grease a 7 by 11 inch pan. Mix the ingredients, except for filling. Mix by hand, or use two knives. Spread half of the mixture in the bottom of the pan. Pack down well. Spread with the date filling. Sprinkle the remaining dough on the top and pat down gently. Bake for 30 minutes. Cut into squares and cool on rack in pan.

NUT BARS (PARVE)

There is no baking required here.

½ c light corn syrup
¼ c brown sugar, packed
¼ tsp salt
1 c peanut butter
1 tsp vanilla
3 c crispy rice cereal
1 c unsalted dry-roasted peanuts

Grease a 7 by 11 inch pan. Mix corn syrup, sugar, and salt in a pot. Heat to boiling. Turn down heat and add peanut butter, mixing well. Remove from heat when smooth, and stir in other ingredients before mixture cools. Turn out into prepared pan, and press down firmly. Chill, then cut into squares. Store in refrigerator.

OATMEAL CHOCOLATE COOKIES (PARVE)

This is another no-bake cookie.

½ c margarine
2 c brown sugar, packed
3 T cocoa powder
1 peeled, grated apple
3 c quick-cooking oats (uncooked)
¼ c chopped walnuts
1 tsp vanilla

In a saucepan, mix and heat margarine, brown sugar, cocoa, and apple. Boil for one minute, stirring. Remove from heat and mix in remaining ingredients. Drop by tablespoonfuls onto waxed paper–lined trays. Chill until firm. Store in refrigerator.

OATMEAL NO-BAKES (PARVE)

If the weather is hot and you don't want to heat up the oven, try making no-bake cookies! This recipe is suitable for children to make.

²/₃ **c margarine at room temperature**
1 c confectioners' sugar
½ tsp vanilla or almond extract
2 c quick-cooking oatmeal (uncooked)

Mix margarine well with sugar. Beat in vanilla and stir in oats. Spread wax paper on a cookie sheet. Drop dough by teaspoonfuls on wax paper and chill until firm. Store in refrigerator.

OATMEAL RAISIN BARS (PARVE)

¾ c shortening
1 c brown sugar, packed
1 tsp vanilla
½ tsp baking soda
½ tsp salt
½ tsp cinnamon
1 egg
1 c all-purpose flour (unsifted)
1½ c quick-cooking oatmeal (uncooked)
½ c chopped walnuts
1 c raisins

Preheat oven to 350°. Grease a 9 by 13 inch pan. Mix together well all ingredients except oats, flour, nuts, and raisins. Stir in flour. Then, add oats, nuts, and raisins, and mix well. Spread in pan and bake 30 minutes. Cut in squares. Cool on rack.

PRUNEDALE BARS (PARVE)

These easy bars are named after the California town of Prunedale, whose inhabitants are proud to be named after this nourishing fruit.

½ c cut-up cooked prunes (about 12)
⅔ c prune juice from cooked prunes
1 egg
¼ c oil
1 c all-purpose flour (unsifted)
⅔ c sugar
½ tsp baking powder
½ tsp salt
½ tsp cinnamon
¼ tsp allspice
nonstick cooking spray or shortening
¼ c confectioners' sugar (optional)

Preheat oven to 375°. Cook prunes in enough water to cover. Allow to cool. Remove pits and cut the prunes up. Place all ingredients in a large bowl. Beat with an electric mixer for 3 minutes or beat well by hand. Spray a 9 by 13 inch pan with nonstick cooking spray, or grease with shortening. Spread batter in pan. Bake 30 minutes, or until done. Cut in bars with serrated knife. Sprinkle bars with confectioners' sugar, if desired.

PRUNE *HAMANTASCHEN* (PARVE)

Purim is not complete without these wonderful, traditional cookies. If your cookies are unfolding during baking, try moistening the edges slightly with water when pinching together.

Filling:
1 lb pitted, diced prunes
½ c orange marmalade

Cook prunes in a small amount of water until tender. Drain and mix with marmalade.

Dough:
¾ c oil
1 c sugar
3 eggs
¼ c warm water
4¾ c all-purpose flour
2 tsp baking powder
½ tsp salt

Blend oil and sugar. Beat in eggs and water. Sift dry ingredients, and combine with egg mixture. Divide pastry into 4 balls. Preheat oven to 375°. Roll out dough on floured board. Cut into circles with cookie cutter and put a spoonful of prune mixture on each. Fold up edges to make triangles, pinching the corners. Bake for 10 to 12 minutes. Cool on racks. Makes 100 cookies or less, depending upon the size of the cookie cutter.

RAISIN COOKIES (PARVE)

This is a bar cookie. I like this type of cookie as they are quicker to make than most other recipes.

1 c raisins
½ c water
½ c margarine at room temperature
1 c sugar
2 eggs
2 c sifted all-purpose flour
1 tsp baking powder
1 tsp cinnamon
1 tsp vanilla

Bring the water to a boil and cook raisins in it for 5 minutes. Cool. Preheat oven to 375°. Grease a 9 by 13 inch pan. Cream margarine with sugar and beat in eggs. Add the raisins and the water they were cooked in. Stir in all other ingredients and mix well. Spread in pan and bake for 20 to 25 minutes, or until done. Cool on a rack and cut into bars.

REFRIGERATOR COOKIES (PARVE)

These cookies are excellent to make for Chanukah or Purim.

1 c margarine at room temperature
1 c sugar
2 eggs
½ tsp vanilla
½ tsp almond flavoring (or 1 tsp vanilla instead of the almond
    and vanilla combination)
1 T molasses
3 c sifted all-purpose flour
3 tsp baking powder
1 tsp salt
¼ c candied cherries, sprinkles, or nuts (optional)

Cream the margarine and sugar together. Add eggs, flavoring, and molasses. Sift the dry ingredients and add. Shape the dough into long rolls, wrapping in waxed paper and chill overnight. The next day, slice into ¼ inch thick slices and bake on greased cookie sheets at 375° for about 8 minutes. May be decorated before baking with candied cherries, sprinkles, or nuts. Makes about 5 dozen cookies.

RICE CEREAL COOKIES (PARVE)

These make a good gift cookie.

¼ c margarine
2 c marshmallow creme
5 c crisp rice cereal

Grease a 9 by 13 inch pan with margarine. Place margarine and marshmallow creme in a large pot and heat, stirring, for about 5 minutes. Remove from heat and mix in the cereal. Press firmly into pan and allow to cool. Cut into squares and refrigerate.

SANDY'S BAR COOKIES (PARVE)

Check to see if the chocolate chips contain milk.

½ c margarine at room temperature
6 T sugar
6 T brown sugar
½ tsp vanilla
1 egg
1 c plus 2 T all-purpose flour (unsifted)
½ tsp baking soda
¼ tsp salt
6 oz chocolate chips
½ c chopped nuts (optional)

Preheat oven to 375°. Grease a 9 inch square pan. Mix margarine with sugars. Add egg and beat well, then stir in vanilla. Mix in remaining ingredients. Spread in pan and bake for 20 to 30 minutes. Cool on a rack and cut into bars.

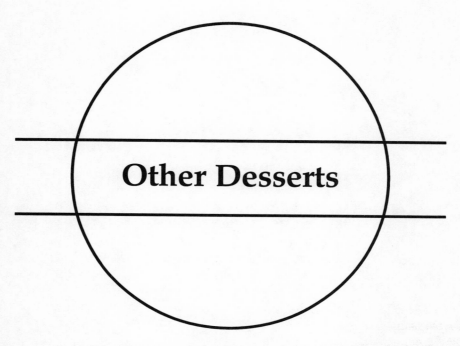

Other Desserts

A good dessert is a gratifying ending to an enjoy-
able meal.

AMBROSIA (PARVE)

In Greek and Roman mythology, ambrosia was the food of "the gods." (It also means something delicious.) So for a kosher cookbook, maybe I should have renamed this recipe something like Tu B'Shevat (New Year of the Trees) Dessert, I guess. Whatever you want to call it, it is simple and refreshing. To be fancy, top with whipped topping and a cherry!

2 oranges, peeled and cut in sections
1 can (8 oz) pineapple, sliced or chunk
1 c shredded coconut
2 T sugar (optional)
1 banana, sliced

Place all ingredients in a bowl, mix, and chill. Serve in individual dishes.

APPLE FLUDEN (PARVE)

A Jewish apple pie. I hope you can get the currants.

Filling:
3 c baking apples, thinly sliced
¾ c sugar
¾ c currants or raisins
⅓ c chopped walnuts
3 T flour
1 tsp cinnamon
¼ tsp allspice

Dough:
2½ c all-purpose flour
2 tsp baking powder
1½ tsp salt
2 eggs
⅓ c oil
⅓ c water
⅓ c sugar
1½ tsp vanilla

Icing:
1 c sifted confectioners' sugar
approximately 2–3 T boiling water
½ tsp vanilla

Prepare filling by mixing the filling ingredients. Sift together the dry
ingredients for the dough. Beat together the other dough ingredients, and combine with the flour mixture to make a dough. Divide
the dough into three portions. Preheat oven to 350° and grease a
9 inch square pan. Roll out one portion of the dough, and line the
pan. Cover with half the filling mixture. Repeat this procedure, and
then top with the last piece of dough. Seal edges, and cut slits in the
top. Bake for 1 hour, or until brown. Place on rack to cool. While
still warm, cover with icing. Allow to cool and cut into squares.

APPLE NOODLE KUGEL (PARVE)

We are lucky that we can buy noodles. They used to be something our grandmothers laboriously made at home; maybe you still do?

8 oz noodles, cooked and drained
2 eggs, beaten
1½ T sugar
½ tsp salt
½ tsp cinnamon
1 c grated apples
¼ c raisins
¼ c chopped walnuts
4 T margarine, cut into pieces

Mix all ingredients together, and put in a greased 9 by 13 inch pan. Bake at 400° for 45 minutes to 1 hour. Serves six.

APPLESAUCE (PARVE)

Applesauce is very necessary for Chanukah as a topping for Potato Latkes; it is also a good recipe for Passover.

4 c chopped cooking apples
2 T lemon juice
1 c water

Stir together in a saucepan, then cover and simmer 10 minutes. Uncover and simmer 10 more minutes, or until apples are tender.

Variation: Add 2 tablespoons sugar and / or ½ teaspoon cinnamon if desired.

BREAD PUDDING (MILK)

This is a rather old-fashioned dessert these days. However, it is still a good way to use leftover bread.

1 egg plus 1 egg white (or use egg substitute)
2 c nonfat (skim) milk
⅓ c sugar
⅛ tsp salt
1 tsp vanilla extract
½ tsp cinnamon
3 slices bread, cubed
¼ c raisins

Heat oven to 350°. Lightly grease the bottom of a 1½ quart glass baking pan. Beat eggs and mix in all other ingredients. Pour into pan and bake for 40 minutes. Serve warm or cold. Serves four.

CHOCOLATE DELIGHT (PARVE)

Try this for an evening when the family is gathered together. It is a super "nosh" (snack).

½ c margarine or butter
¾ c sugar
⅓ c cocoa powder
¼ c all-purpose flour (unsifted)
2 eggs
1 tsp vanilla

Preheat oven to 350°. Grease a 9 inch pie pan. Melt margarine in a saucepan. Remove from heat and stir in sugar, cocoa powder, and flour. Add eggs and vanilla and beat well. Pour into the prepared pan and bake for 15 minutes. Cool on a rack, and then cut into wedges. Serves six.

GELATIN PIE (PARVE)

1 baked or graham cracker pie crust
1 pkg (3 oz) kosher gelatin (any flavor)
boiling water
1½ c chopped, drained fruit, such as canned pears, peaches, fruit
cocktail, sliced banana, or strawberries
whipped cream or substitute topping

Prepare gelatin by mixing with boiling water, as directed on the package. Chill. When the gelatin is thickened but not too firm, mix in the fruit and pour into the pie crust. Chill. Serve with cream or substitute topping.

GREEN APPLE PIE (PARVE)

This pie is a good dessert for a Thanksgiving or Chanukah dinner.

2 lb green apples
pastry for a 2 crust pie
¾ c sugar
½ tsp cinnamon
¼ tsp nutmeg
⅛ tsp salt
1 tsp grated lemon peel
2 T margarine

Line a 9 inch pie pan with pastry. Peel apples and slice thinly. Mix together the sugar, spices, salt, and lemon peel. Put half of the apples in the pie pan, and sprinkle with half the sugar mixture. Add the rest of the apples, and sprinkle with the rest of the sugar. Dot with the margarine. Add top crust, seal edges, and cut slits in the top. Bake at 425° for 40 minutes.

HAWAIIAN PINEAPPLE MERINGUE PIE (PARVE)

1 baked or graham cracker pie shell
1 T margarine
1 tsp grated lemon rind
1 T lemon juice
4 tsp potato starch
3 T sugar
¼ tsp salt
1 can (20 oz) crushed pineapple in its own juice

Meringue:
2 egg whites
4 T sugar

Prepare and set aside the margarine, lemon rind, and juice. In a saucepan, mix together the potato starch, 3 tablespoons sugar, and salt. Add pineapple (including the juice) and cook, stirring, over medium heat until thickened. Remove from heat and stir in margarine, lemon rind, and juice. Cool slightly and then spread in pie shell. Preheat oven to 400°. To make the meringue, beat egg whites until foamy, then gradually beat in the 4 tablespoons sugar. When egg whites are stiff, spread over the pie filling, sealing to the edges. Bake about 5 minutes, until lightly browned.

LEMON CREAM PIE (MILK)

This recipe breaks my rule about not having to separate eggs, but at least the whites don't have to be beaten or anything. They can be cooked into an omelet, meringue, or something later! And this is a very easy and tasty pie.

1 graham cracker crust or baked pastry shell
3 egg yolks
1 tsp grated lemon peel (just the yellow part)
1 can (14 oz) sweetened, condensed milk (*not* evaporated milk)
½ c lemon juice (takes about 3 lemons)
whipped cream or substitute topping

Preheat oven to 325°. Beat together the egg yolks and grated lemon peel for 2 minutes. Add condensed milk and lemon juice and beat for 2 minutes more. Pour into pie crust and bake for 30 minutes. Allow to cool on a rack. Chill and store in refrigerator. Serve topped with the whipped cream.

PETER PUMPKIN EATER (MILK)

3 eggs, beaten (or egg substitute)
¾ c honey
½ tsp ginger
1 tsp cinnamon
¼ tsp salt
1 can (16 oz) pumpkin
1 c canned, evaporated, low-fat milk
whipped cream or substitute topping (optional)

Preheat oven to 325°. Mix eggs, honey, spices, salt, and pumpkin. Stir in milk. Grease the bottom of a 9 inch pie pan, preferably one with high sides. Pour custard into pan and bake 1 hour, or until a silver knife inserted in the center comes out clean. Cool on rack and chill before serving in wedges. May be topped with whipped cream when serving. Serves four to six.

RICE PUDDING (MILK)

This pudding is easy to make. It is not very sweet, so if you like sweet desserts, add a little more sugar. You may substitute 2 cups of left-over cooked rice for uncooked rice and water.

1 c rice, uncooked
2 c water
2 c milk
2 eggs, beaten
⅓ c sugar
½ c raisins
1 tsp vanilla
1 apple, peeled and grated
1 T margarine or butter
1 tsp cinnamon

Put rice and water in a covered saucepan and bring to a boil. Lower heat to simmer, cover tightly, and cook for 20 minutes. Remove from heat and allow rice to cool. Preheat oven to 350°. Grease a 9 by 12 inch pan. Stir milk and eggs into the rice. Add sugar, raisins, vanilla, and apple. Mix well and pour into pan. Dot with the margarine and sprinkle with cinnamon. Bake 1 hour, until edges are golden and a silver knife inserted in the center comes out clean. Cool and chill. Serves eight.

EASY PIE CRUST (PARVE)

This is not only easy, it is low in cholesterol.

Single crust (9 inch pie pan):
1¹/₃ c sifted all-purpose flour
½ tsp salt
¹/₃ c salad oil
2 T cold water

Double crust:
2 c sifted all-purpose flour
1 tsp salt (or a little less)
½ c salad oil
3 T cold water

Mix flour, salt, and oil. Stir well with a fork. Sprinkle with the water, and mix well. Flatten ball with your hands. (If making a double crust, make into two balls.) Place dough between two pieces of waxed paper and roll out with a rolling pin until large enough to fit a 9 inch pie pan (start rolling from center). Remove top piece of paper and invert over pie pan. Remove second paper, and patch crust if necessary. For a single-size crust, prick bottom several times with a fork and bake at 450° for 12 to 15 minutes, until browned. For a double crust, roll out second pastry and place on top of filling. Remove paper, cut slits in top, and bake as directed in a pie recipe.

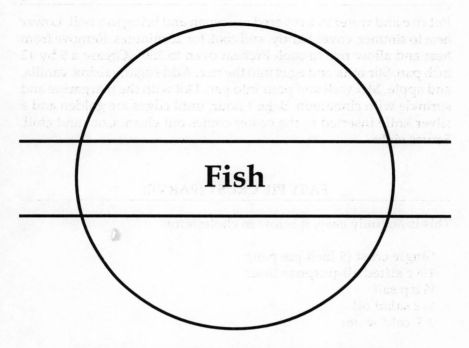

Fish

Fish is easy to cook. Depending upon your recipe, it can be quite low in calories. It should not be over-cooked. Serve promptly when done.

BAKED FISH FILLETS

I learned this recipe soon after my husband and I married, and it has remained one of our favorites.

1 large onion, diced
2 ribs celery, sliced
1 or 2 lb fish fillets
1 can (15 oz) tomato sauce
1 T oil
1 tsp dried parsley flakes or 1 T fresh parsley, chopped
½ tsp salt (optional)
dash pepper
1 tsp paprika

Grease or spray with nonstick spray a 9 by 13 inch pan. Put onions and celery in the bottom. Place fish over the vegetables. Pour tomato sauce and oil over the top and add seasonings. Bake at 375° for 30 minutes, or until the fish flakes easily with a fork. Serves four to six.

BAKED SALMON (MILK)

Salmon is a large and delicious fish. This recipe is suitable for Passover.

   1½ lb of whole salmon
   salt and pepper
   1 clove garlic
   1 small onion, sliced
   ½ c milk
   1 T margarine
   1 tsp dried parsley flakes, or 1 T chopped, fresh parsley

Place all ingredients in a pan. Cover and bake at 400° for about 30 minutes (depending on thickness of fish), until fish flakes easily with a fork. Serves three to four.

BAKED TROUT

Trout is a favorite freshwater game fish, but the ones in the market come from fish farms. This recipe is suitable for Passover.

   1 whole, cleaned trout
   lemon
   1 T margarine or oil

Heat oven to 450°. Place trout in a baking pan. Put a lemon slice inside the fish and squeeze some lemon juice over it. Top fish with margarine or brush with oil. Bake 10 to 20 minutes—according to size of fish. Fish is done when it flakes easily with a fork. One large trout serves two; two small ones will serve three.

BOILED FISH

Some types of fish are better when simmered in water than cooked by any other method. See the Salad Dressings and Sauces chapter for the Tartar Sauce recipe.

1 whole fish or large slice of fish
1 lemon, sliced
1 tsp parsley flakes, or 1 T chopped fresh parsley
1 tsp pickling spices (optional)
1–2 slices onion
1 rib celery, sliced
hot water

Place fish in a large pan with other ingredients. Cover with the hot water. Simmer for 10 minutes per pound of fish. Drain. Serve with mayonnaise or Tartar Sauce. Serves two per pound.

CREAMED FISH (MILK)

Use leftover or canned fish. Serve with rice. This is quick to make. Fresh green beans, cut up, can be used instead of the frozen vegetables.

2 T oil or margarine
1 small onion, sliced
2 c cubed, leftover fish
1 tsp parsley flakes
½ tsp tarragon
dash of pepper
½ tsp salt, or to taste
¼–½ tsp cumin (optional)
1 c frozen mixed vegetables or leftover vegetables
1 c milk (may be nonfat)
2 tsp potato starch

Heat oil, and cook the onion until it goes limp. Add the fish, parsley, tarragon, salt, pepper, and cumin, and stir. Stir in the vegetables and milk. Cook and stir over medium to low heat until vegetables are about done. Mix the potato starch with 2 tablespoons cold water. Stir in and cook until sauce thickens. Serves three to four.

CRISPY BAKED FISH FILLETS (MILK)

Lovely served with Tartar Sauce or ketchup.

1 lb fish fillets
2 T oil
½ c milk
½ c fine bread crumbs or corn flake crumbs
½ tsp salt or seasoned salt
dash of pepper

Heat oven to 375°. Put oil in the bottom of a shallow baking pan. Dip fish in milk, then roll in the crumbs. Place in the baking pan and sprinkle with the seasonings. Bake for 15 to 20 minutes, or until fish is easily flaked with a fork. Serves four.

ESTHER'S POACHED FISH

More herbs may be added, if desired, such as ½ teaspoon thyme or tarragon. This recipe is suitable for Passover.

1–2 lb of fish, whole or fillet
2 c water
2 T lemon juice
½ small onion, chopped
1 clove garlic, minced
½ tsp salt (optional)
dash of pepper
1 tsp dried parsley or 1 T chopped, fresh parsley
1 T chopped celery tops (optional)

Clean fish. Combine ingredients, except fish, in a large skillet. Place fish into mixture. Cover and bring to boil. Lower heat, and simmer for about 20 minutes, depending on size of fish, until it flakes easily with a fork. Serves four to six.

FILLETS IN VEGETABLE SAUCE

Good with rice or boiled or mashed potatoes.

½ lb fish fillets (such as sole or red snapper)
1 T margarine
1 small onion, sliced
1 clove garlic, minced
1 small zucchini, sliced
1 small eggplant, sliced (optional)
1 rib celery, sliced
2 T flour
½ c water
1 small tomato, diced
½ tsp basil
dash of cumin or curry powder
salt and pepper to taste

In a large skillet, heat margarine. Add vegetables, except tomato, and cook over medium high heat until onion begins to brown. Stir in flour; then gradually mix in water. A sauce will form. Turn heat down to simmer, and top vegetables with fish and tomato. Add seasonings. Cover and simmer until fish is tender, adding a little extra water if necessary. Serves two to three.

FISH CAKES

Here is an old standby recipe for using up leftover fish and potatoes. This recipe is suitable for Passover.

1½ c cooked fish, cut up or flaked
3 cooked potatoes, mashed
dash of pepper
½ tsp salt (optional)
1 egg, beaten
½ c matzo meal or fine bread crumbs
2 T oil

Mix the fish, potatoes, salt, pepper, and egg. Form into cakes and roll in matzo meal. Fry in the oil, browning on both sides. Serves three to four.

Variations: (1) Add 1 tablespoon grated onion. (2) Instead of frying, place on a greased pan, or one coated with nonstick spray. Bake at 350° for 30 minutes, turning once.

FISH IN SAUCE

Good with rice.

2 T margarine or butter
1 large onion, chopped
1 green pepper, sliced (optional)
1 garlic clove, minced
1 rib celery, sliced
2 T flour
½ c water
1 tsp seasoned salt
pepper to taste
½ tsp curry powder
2 c frozen green peas
1 lb fish fillets

Heat margarine in a large skillet. Add onion, green pepper, garlic, and celery. Cook, stirring, until onion starts to brown. Turn heat down to medium low. Stir in flour and mix well. Gradually add water, stirring until sauce forms. Stir in seasonings and top with peas and fish. Cover and simmer until fish is tender, adding a small amount of additional water if necessary. Serves four.

FISH STEW

1½ lb fish fillets
1 small summer squash, quartered
1 small eggplant, diced
1 small onion, sliced

1 carrot, sliced
1 small tomato, diced
1 rib celery, sliced
salt and pepper to taste
1–2 c water

Place all ingredients in a pot and heat to boiling. Lower heat and simmer for 30 minutes, or until tender. Serves four.

MARION'S FISH BROIL

1 lb fish fillets
2 T squeezable margarine
juice of ½ lemon

Heat barbecue or broiler. Turn heat lower, or use a high rack. Place fish over coals or on broiler, and baste with margarine and lemon juice. Turn fish once. Fish is done when it flakes easily with a fork. Do not overcook. Serves three or four.

SALMON CAKES

Nothing in the house to eat? How about a can of salmon?

1 can (15 oz) salmon, or use 2 c cooked, fresh salmon
dash of pepper
2 tsp dried onion flakes or ¼ c grated onion
2 eggs, beaten
2 tsp lemon juice
3 T fine bread crumbs
½ c matzo meal or bread crumbs
2 T oil

Drain salmon and mash. Mix with pepper, onion, eggs, lemon juice, and 3 tablespoons bread crumbs. Form into patties and roll in the ½ cup matzo meal or crumbs. Heat oil in skillet, and fry until browned on both sides. Serves three to four.

SALMON LOAF (MILK)

1 can (15 oz) salmon
1 T lemon juice
½ tsp salt
dash of pepper
2 eggs, beaten
1 rib celery, diced
2 slices white bread, crumbled
½ tsp baking powder
1 c evaporated milk (may be evaporated skim milk)

Grease a 1½ quart loaf pan. Set oven at 350°. Drain and mash salmon.
Mix in other ingredients, and pour into pan. Bake for about 35 minutes, or until firm. Serves four.

TOMATO, TUNA, AND NOODLES

2 T margarine
1 small onion, diced
2 tsp dried parsley flakes
1 can (14½ oz) stewed tomatoes
3 c cooked noodles (5 oz uncooked)
1 can (6 oz) tuna, drained and flaked
8 oz frozen, mixed vegetables
pepper
½ tsp basil
bread crumbs (1 slice bread, cubed)

Boil some water and cook the noodles. Meanwhile, using a pot that
can go from the top of the stove into the oven, melt the margarine
and cook the onion until it starts to brown. Add the tomatoes and
frozen vegetables. Heat to boiling. Turn down the heat and simmer
until vegetables are tender. Drain cooked noodles and add to tomatoes and onions, along with all other ingredients except the crumbs.
Stir and top with crumbs. Bake at 375° for 20 minutes. Serves three.

TUNA CURRY

Serve with rice.

1 large onion, chopped
1 large apple, peeled and grated
2 T margarine or butter
1 T curry powder (or more, to taste)
1 can (16 oz) tomatoes
1 can (12 oz) tuna

In a large frying pan, heat the margarine and cook the onion and apple. Add the curry and the whole can of tomatoes, cutting up the tomatoes. Bring to boil, lower heat, and simmer for 20 minutes. Add the tuna and cook 5 minutes longer. Serves four.

TUNA NOODLE CASSEROLE (MILK)

There are no difficult sauces to mix, and ¾ cup leftover fish can be substituted for the tuna.

6 oz noodles, cooked and drained
2 T margarine
1 onion, chopped
1 c vegetables: peas, carrots, or green beans, either raw,
    frozen, or canned
1 can (6 oz) tuna, drained
½ tsp salt
pepper to taste
½ tsp thyme
1 c milk
⅓ c instant mashed potato flakes
1 slice of buttered bread, cubed (optional)
1 or 2 slices American cheese (optional)

Preheat oven to 350°. Brown the onion in margarine. Add vegetables and heat. Stir in tuna, salt, pepper, thyme, and milk. Heat, then mix in the potato flakes. Layer noodles and tuna mixture in a casserole. Top with the bread cubes, the cheese, or both if desired. Bake for 20 minutes. Serves three or four.

TURBOT CASSEROLE

1½ lb turbot (or flounder) fillets
1 can (16 oz) tomatoes, sliced
1 tsp garlic or onion salt
1 T chopped fresh parsley

Cut fish into serving-sized pieces. Place all ingredients in a casserole. Bake in 400° oven for 20 to 30 minutes, or until fish flakes easily with a fork. Serves six.

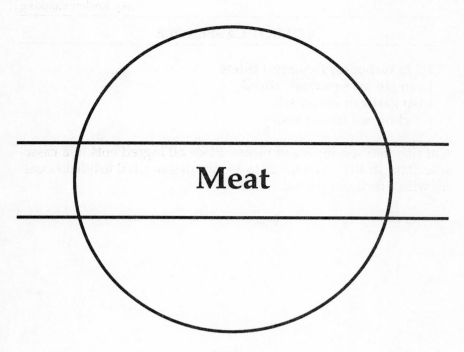

Meat

Menu

When our budget needs a stretch,
Tuna fish is what I fetch.

When the paycheck takes a squeeze,
There is macaroni and some cheese.

When the wallet's getting thin,
We eat something from a tin.

When we do not want to beg,
Then we scramble up an egg.

But of all the meals we eat,
My family prefers some meat.

BAKED VEAL BREAST

This is a really easy recipe. A three-pound breast of veal serves five or six.

1 breast of veal
½ c water
½ tsp garlic salt
¹/₈ tsp dry mustard
½ tsp celery seed

Heat oven to 325°. Place veal in a large pan. Add all ingredients. Cover and bake 30 to 35 minutes *per pound*.

BEEF STEW

This is not only superb on a cold day, but you can add a few more
potatoes and extra meat to serve a crowd.

1 T oil
1 lb beef stew meat
1 medium onion
1–2 cloves garlic, minced
1 c water
2–3 potatoes
2–3 carrots
1–2 parsnips (optional)
½ bell pepper
1 rib celery
1 turnip (optional)
2 sprigs parsley or 1 tsp dried parsley
1 tsp rosemary
1 tsp thyme
½ tsp marjoram
1 can (8 oz) tomato sauce
salt and pepper, to taste
½ c frozen mixed vegetables

Brown beef, onion, and garlic in the oil. Drain off excess fat. Peel
and dice the vegetables. Add all ingredients except frozen vegetables, and heat to boiling. Lower heat and simmer 1½ or 2 hours,
or until beef is tender. Add frozen vegetables and cook ten minutes
longer. Serves four.

Variation: Add other vegetables, such as ½ cup cabbage, green
beans, or summer squash, near the end of the cooking time.

BRAISED CHUCK STEAK

Chuck steak can be tough if not cooked slowly and gently.

1 T oil
1¼ lb chuck steak
1 T flour

1 clove garlic, minced (optional)
2 onions, sliced
½ tsp marjoram
4 carrots, sliced
2–3 potatoes, peeled and sliced
1 c water
pepper and salt, to taste

Heat oil in a large pan. Coat meat with the flour and brown in the oil. Add garlic and onion, and brown along with the meat. Add other ingredients and bring to a boil. Turn down the heat. Cover and simmer on low heat for 1½ hours, or until meat and vegetables are tender. Serves three to four.

BRISKET OF BEEF

The size of the cut of beef will determine your cooking time. Never rush a brisket; it will be tender if cooked at a low heat. How you slice the cooked meat is important—slice across the grain. Don't be tempted to slice along the strings of the beef, or it will be harder to chew and seem tough.

Brisket is often served on Chanukah with latkes. My brother-in-law Jeff would never be satisfied with anything else. This recipe is also suitable for Passover.

beef brisket, 4 lbs or more
¼ c water
1 onion, cut in half
4 or more carrots, peeled
4 or more potatoes, peeled and cut in half
1 garlic clove (optional)

Place brisket in a roasting pan with the water and onion. Cover and cook in a 325° oven for 1 hour. Turn over the meat and add the vegetables. Add more water if necessary. Cover and cook until beef and vegetables are tender—at least 1 more hour.

BROILED LAMB CHOPS

My friend, Judy, once told me about the first meal she cooked for her husband, Tony. "I rushed home from work, and cooked peas and lamb chops. They came out great, but Tony didn't arrive home from work for another hour and a half. I hate to tell you what they looked like by then!"

Have the rest of the meal prepared and the family just about sitting around the table before you broil the chops. It is a good idea to serve soup or a salad for people to munch on while the chops cook.

This recipe is suitable for Passover.

1 lamb chop for each person

Heat broiler. Place chops on broiler and brown well on each side. Lamb chops take about 10 minutes to broil, depending on size and thickness.

BUBBLE AND SQUEAK

This is the name of an English dish—a fun name for fried leftovers! Actually, I learned this recipe when I was a little girl. My baby-sitter took me along with her for a visit with a friend of hers, who was a cook on a small ship. As we stood chatting in the galley, she made this dish.

I often make Bubble and Squeak on Passover, using leftover turkey or chicken. Feel free to vary the amounts of the ingredients according to the leftovers available.

1 onion
1–2 c diced leftover potatoes and other cooked vegetables from a roast, such as turnips, carrots
1–2 c leftover beef, cut in cubes
2 T oil for frying

Heat oil in a large, heavy skillet. Dice the onion, and while it is cooking, cut up and add other ingredients. Turn with a spatula. Cook until hot and browned on the edges. Serve with ketchup and pickles. Serves three or four.

Variation: Use leftover turkey or chicken instead of beef.

CHILI WITH MEAT

If you like hot food, add more spice to your chili. Serve with crackers, bread, or tortillas.

1 T oil
1 small onion, diced
½ lb hamburger meat
1–2 diced green peppers (fresh or frozen)
1 can (15 oz) cooked kidney or pinto beans, or 2½ c home-cooked
**   beans**
1 tsp chili powder (or to taste)
1 can (8 oz) tomato sauce

Heat oil in large skillet. Add onions and cook over medium heat about 5 minutes, or until onions become soft and clear. Add meat and stir until it browns. Add other ingredients and simmer 10 minutes. Serves two to three.

CHOLENT

This famous recipe is hundreds of years old. It was especially popular in Europe during the cold winter months. People would arrange with the local baker to use his oven for this slow-cooking bean dish. The plan was to have a hot, nourishing meal for the Sabbath. I have included a meatless version in the Vegetarian Main Dishes chapter.

1 c dried beans (kidney beans, lima beans, garbanzos, great
**   northerns, or any combination of these)**
2 T oil
1 lb beef (brisket, flanken, chuck, stew meat, or hamburger
**   meat)**
1 T flour
2 onions, sliced
salt and pepper
4–6 potatoes, cut in chunks
½ c pearl barley
1 tsp paprika
boiling water
1 clove garlic, minced (optional)

Wash beans, cover with water, and bring to a boil. Boil 5 minutes. Turn off heat and allow to soak, covered, for 1 hour. Heat oil in a large, heavy pot. Coat meat in flour, and brown in the oil. (If using hamburger, stir to brown, drain off any excess fat, and stir in the flour.) Stir in onions and cook until browned. Mix in all other ingredients, cover with boiling water, and bring to a boil. Add dumplings, if desired. Cover and bake at 325° for 3 to 4 hours, or until meat and beans are tender. May be cooked in a Crock-Pot, on low, for 11 to 12 hours. Sometimes it is also cooked on top of the stove, on a special burner cover, for many hours. Do not stir, but shake the pan occasionally, adding a little more water if necessary. Serves six.

Variation: Add carrots, turnips, parsley, garlic, or marjoram. For a quicker-cooking version, use some leftover meat and canned beans.

Dumplings (*Knaidle*) (Parve)

This dumpling recipe is good with any stew or most soups.

1 c sifted all-purpose flour
½ tsp salt
2 tsp baking powder
1 T shortening
½ c water (approximately)

Mix dry ingredients. Cut in shortening with two knives or pastry blender. Gradually mix in water, until a thick batter is formed. Drop by tablespoons into boiling food (soup or stew). Turn heat down, but keep the food simmering briskly. Cover tightly and cook about 20 minutes.

CLOCK STEAK

1 lb beef chuck steak
2 T oil
1 clove of garlic, minced
½ c chopped green pepper

salt and pepper to taste
1 onion, sliced
1 can (14½ oz) stewed tomatoes
1 c water
1 rib celery, diced
1 tsp parsley flakes

Brown beef and garlic in the oil, in a dutch oven or large pot with a cover. Add all other ingredients. Cover and bake at 350° for about 2 hours, turning meat a few times during cooking. Serves three to four.

CORNED BEEF OR CORNED TONGUE

I make corned beef or corned tongue in a covered enamel pot, which I place in the refrigerator. Use 1 whole beef tongue or about 10 pounds brisket.

2 c kosher salt
4 c water
1 tsp saltpeter
¼ c sugar
1 T pickling spices
7 bay leaves
1 tsp paprika
6 cloves garlic, sliced

Boil brine ingredients except the garlic. Allow to cool. Place about 10 pounds of brisket or tongue in pot, and cover with the brine. Add garlic and more water if necessary. Put a plate on top to hold meat down under the brine. Turn meat over every week. Pickle for about 3 weeks.

To cook: remove from brine and rinse under running water. Place in a large pot, cover with water, and bring to boil. Lower heat and simmer for 3 or more hours, until meat is tender. Cool slightly, and carefully slice brisket across the grain. If making tongue, peel and slice after cooking and allowing to cool.

Corned Beef and Cabbage

Add these vegetables or some combination of them 30 minutes before the end of cooking:

6 carrots
1 rutabaga, diced
6 small potatoes
3 medium onions
1 cabbage, quartered

CROCK-POT STEW

A good dish to serve on a cold winter day. Add salt when serving, if desired. Never serve a bay leaf—always remove it from the food. It adds flavor but is fibrous, and therefore indigestible.

3 potatoes, sliced
2 lb stewing beef
1 small turnip, peeled and diced (optional)
3–4 carrots, diced
1 small yam, peeled and diced
1 small onion, diced
1 T Worcestershire sauce
1 clove garlic, minced
1 c water
1 sprig parsley
dash of pepper
½ green pepper, sliced
1 tsp rosemary
½ bay leaf

Place all ingredients in order given into Crock-Pot. Cover and cook on high for 2 hours. Turn heat to low and let simmer for 5 to 6 more hours. Remove bay leaf before serving. Serves six.

FRESH TONGUE

beef tongue
1 bay leaf
1 onion, sliced
1 tsp whole pepper corns or pickling spices

Clean tongue. Place all ingredients in large pot, and cover with water. Bring to a boil, lower heat, and simmer until tongue is tender (about 3 hours). Cool, peel, and slice the tongue.

GOULASH IN THE OVEN

Serve with boiled noodles or mashed potatoes.

1½ lb beef, cut in cubes
1 large onion, sliced
3 carrots, sliced
1 rib celery, sliced
2 cloves garlic, minced
½ bell pepper, sliced
1 tsp paprika
1 tsp dried parsley flakes or 1 T chopped fresh parsley
1 can (15 oz) tomato sauce
¼ c water
3 drops red pepper sauce or ⅛ tsp red pepper
dash of salt (optional)
½ tsp basil

Place all ingredients in a covered casserole and bake at 325° for 1½ to 2 hours—until meat is tender. Serves four to six.

GROUND BEEF AND NOODLES

Start cooking noodles as you cook the meat.

1 lb ground beef
1 onion, diced
1 clove garlic, minced
1 T oil
1 rib celery, diced
salt and pepper
½ tsp cumin
2 c water
1 c frozen mixed vegetables
8 oz noodles (cooked)

Brown beef, onion, and garlic in oil, stirring well. If necessary, drain off excess fat. Add celery, salt and pepper, and cumin. Add water and bring to boil. Lower heat and simmer for 15 minutes. Add the frozen vegetables and cook 10 minutes, or until vegetables are cooked. Serve with cooked noodles.

HAMBURGERS

Hamburgers may be cooked medium or well done, depending on taste. Serve on a plate of vegetables or in hamburger buns. Popular toppings for hamburgers are ketchup, mustard, pickles, onion slices, lettuce, tomato, and Thousand Island dressing. A California Burger has Guacamole on top. Good accompaniments for hamburgers are fried potatoes, coleslaw, baked beans, salads, and fried onions.

1 lb ground hamburger

Broiled Hamburgers: Place patties on a hot barbecue grill or a broiler and cook until browned, turning once. For plain hamburgers, form ground beef into patties. One pound will make 4 or 5 good-sized burgers. If you are serving children, you may want to make smaller patties instead.

Grilled Hamburgers: Heat a large frying pan and sprinkle with salt, or add 1 tablespoon oil. Cook burgers until done, turning once.

HOT DOGS

Hot dogs may be eaten plain, on a plate, or in hot dog buns. Hot dogs in buns are often served with mustard, ketchup, and pickle relish. New York-style dogs are served in a bun with mustard and sauerkraut. California Chili Dogs are served in a bun with chili on top. Good accompaniments for hot dogs are potato salad, coleslaw, macaroni salad, french fries, and baked beans.

1 pkg hot dogs

Boiled Hot Dogs: Cover hot dogs with water. Cover pot and bring to a boil. When water is bubbling vigorously, turn off heat and let set 5 minutes.

Broiled Hot Dogs: Score hot dogs, by slitting with a knife diagonally. Place on hot barbecue grill or on broiler and cook until browned, about 5 minutes.

Fried Hot Dogs: Cut hot dogs in half lengthwise or into slices. Fry in 1 tablespoon oil until browned.

Franks and Beans: Cut hot dogs in slices, and add a can of baked beans. Heat and serve. Allow 2 hot dogs and ½ can beans per person.

HUNGARIAN GOULASH

Good with noodles or mashed potatoes.

2 lb lean beef, cubed
2 T oil
2 onions, sliced
1 clove of garlic, minced
2 tsp paprika
1 tsp salt
1 tsp marjoram
1 can (8 oz) tomato sauce
2 tsp soup powder or 2 bouillon cubes
2½ c water

Heat oil in a large skillet or pot that has a cover. Add meat, onions, and garlic; brown, stirring frequently. Drain off excess fat, if any.

Add all other ingredients and heat to boiling. Lower heat to simmer and cook for 1½ hours, or until the meat is tender. Skim off the fat before serving. Serves five.

LAMB SHANKS WITH BEANS

1 can (15 oz) white beans (drained) or 2 c cooked beans
3 lamb shanks
1 T tomato paste
½ tsp celery seeds
½ tsp sugar
1 T oil
1 medium onion, diced
2 cloves garlic, minced
½ tsp oregano
dash of pepper
½ tsp salt
1 tsp soup powder or 1 bouillon cube
1 c hot water

Place beans in a casserole and top with lamb shanks. Add all other ingredients and cover. Bake at 325° for about 1½ hours. After the first ½ hour, turn meat and add more water if necessary. Uncover for last 20 to 30 minutes of cooking. Serves three.

LAMB SHANKS WITH CARROTS

4 lamb shanks
1 can (14½ oz) stewed tomatoes
2 c hot water
1 tsp salt
2 tsp paprika
7 carrots, peeled and cut in large chunks

Place lamb shanks in a large casserole and add all ingredients except carrots. Cover and bake in a 375° oven for ½ hour. Turn meat over and bake for ½ hour more. Then add carrots. Bake, covered, for ½ hour more, or until meat is tender. Serves four.

LAMB STEW

1½ lb lamb neck with bone
1 T flour
1 T oil
1 c water
salt and pepper to taste
3 potatoes, diced
4 carrots, diced
3 parsnips or turnips, diced
1 onion, quartered
1 tsp dried parsley flakes or 1 T chopped fresh parsley
1 tsp basil
2 c frozen green beans or peas

Heat oil in large pot. Dip lamb in flour and brown in hot oil. Add salt, pepper, and water. Cover and bring to boil. Lower heat and simmer for 1 hour. Add potatoes, carrots, parsnips or turnips, onion, parsley, and basil. Simmer 30 minutes more. Add green beans or peas and cook 15 minutes longer, or until meat and vegetables are tender. Serves four to five.

LIVER

Liver has a bad name these days—it has lots of cholesterol. But it is very nourishing, loaded with iron and vitamins. When my children were small and got colds, I would thaw that package of liver I kept in my freezer. The children began to look forward to liver as a treat they got when they were sick, and sure enough, that liver dinner seemed to give them strength. Never mind Popeye's spinach!

1–2 lb liver—either chicken, calf, or sliced beef
1–2 tsp salt

Line your broiler with foil and preheat it. Wash the liver under running cold water. Cut some crisscross lines on the liver with a knife kept especially for liver. Sprinkle with salt, then broil the liver. It takes very little time to cook, so be prepared—just watch closely, and turn the liver to cook on the other side. Wash off blood before serving. Serves four to six.

Chopped Liver

Here's how to use up the leftover liver. My Aunt Lil once prepared chopped liver salads as an appetizer for guests and set them all out on the dining room table. But, before the guests walked into the dining room, the children had gone around the table and eaten the chopped liver off of every plate!

1 hard cooked egg
½ small onion
½–1 lb cooked beef liver or chicken liver
salt and pepper
2 T mayonnaise (or to taste)

Chop up the egg, onion, and liver. Add seasonings and mayonnaise to taste. Serve on lettuce, or with rounds of rye bread. Makes a delicious sandwich, too.

MEAT LOAF SPAGHETTI

This recipe will fit nicely into an electric frying pan, if you have one.

¾ lb hamburger meat
1 egg, beaten, or equivalent egg substitute
½ c bread or cracker crumbs, or matzo meal
1 T oil
1 onion, diced
2 cloves garlic, minced
salt and pepper to taste
1 can (15 oz) tomato sauce
1 tsp oregano
¼ c chopped mushrooms or bell peppers (optional)
8 oz spaghetti (cooked)

Mix meat, egg, and crumbs and shape into patties. Heat oil in a large pan. Brown the patties, turning to brown on both sides. Brown the onion and garlic at the same time. Pour or spoon off any excess fat. Turn heat down, and add salt and pepper, tomato sauce and oregano. Add mushrooms or bell pepper, if desired. Cover and simmer ½ hour, or until patties are done. Serve with spaghetti. Serves three.

Meat Loaf without the Spaghetti

Follow the recipe for Meat Loaf with Spaghetti and shape into patties or a loaf. To cook in the electric frying pan, omit the tomato sauce and oregano. The onions, mushrooms, bell peppers, and garlic are optional. Add 1 teaspoon soup powder or a bouillon cube and ½ cup of hot water or ½ cup leftover soup. Cover and simmer for ½ hour, or until done.

To cook in the oven, place the meat mixture in a greased loaf pan, top with 2 or 3 slices onion if desired, and bake at 350° for ½ hour or until done.

See Meat Loaf Sandwich, in the Sandwich chapter, for an idea for serving leftover Meat Loaf.

MEAT PATTIES

2 slices parve (containing no milk) bread
½ c water
1 egg, beaten
1 lb ground beef
½ tsp salt
dash of pepper
dash of seasoned salt
1 large onion, diced
1 clove garlic, minced
2 T oil

Soak the bread in the water in a large bowl and mash. Add the egg, beef, and seasonings, and mix. Heat the oil in a large skillet. Brown the onion and garlic in the oil. Form the beef mixture into large meatballs, and brown along with the onions. Turn the beef to brown on each side. Lower the heat and cover the pan. Cook slowly on low heat for 30 to 40 minutes, adding a little water if necessary, until done. Serves four.

MEAT-STUFFED GREEN PEPPERS

This recipe makes a one-dish meal. Try to use a pot that is the right size to just accommodate the peppers in an upright position, with a little room between them for the liquid.

4 medium-sized green peppers
¾ lb ground beef (or use ground turkey)
½ c instant rice (brown or white), or an equal amount of cooked
   rice may be substituted
1 clove garlic, minced
1 small onion, chopped fine
salt and pepper
¼ tsp paprika
¼ tsp curry powder
2 c chopped tomatoes or 1 can (16 oz) of tomatoes, sliced
1 tsp Worcestershire sauce
water

Cut tops off the peppers and clean out the seeds with a big spoon. Mix the beef, rice, garlic, onion, salt, and pepper. Fill peppers with the mixture and place in a pan. Put the cut-off tops of the peppers back on them. Add the other ingredients to the pan, along with just enough water to reach to the tops of the peppers. Cover the pan and bring to a boil. Turn heat to medium low, and simmer, covered, about 1 hour, or until peppers are tender and meat is done. Serves two to four.

MOUSSAKA

Nice served with rice.

1 large eggplant or zucchini
¼ c oil
1 large onion, diced
1 clove garlic, minced
1 lb ground beef, turkey, or lamb
¼ c green pepper, chopped
1 can (16 oz) tomatoes

1 can (8 oz) tomato sauce
salt and pepper to taste
1 tsp parsley flakes or 1 T chopped fresh parsley
¼ tsp marjoram

Slice eggplant and brown lightly in oil. Remove from pan, and brown onion and garlic. Add ground meat and green pepper, and stir until meat begins to brown. Remove any excess fat from pan. Add tomatoes and seasonings. Heat oven to 350°. Layer eggplant and sauce in a greased casserole, or one sprayed with nonstick spray, ending with sauce on top. Cover and bake 50 to 60 minutes. Serves four.

Variation: Instead of sauteing the eggplant, cook the slices, on a Teflon or nonstick-sprayed pan, in the oven at 350° for 30 minutes, turning once.

OSSO BUCO—ITALIAN VEAL SHANKS

This sounds fancy, and it *is* fancy, but it is just as easy to make as a beef stew. Serve with rice.

3 T oil
2 carrots, sliced (optional)
1 small onion, diced
1 garlic clove, minced
1 rib celery, sliced
2 veal shanks
¼ c flour
salt and pepper to taste
2 slices lemon
1 tsp parsley flakes (or 1 T chopped fresh parsley)
1 c water (or white wine)
1 can (14½ oz) stewed tomatoes
½ tsp oregano
½ tsp basil

Heat oil in a large pan with a cover. Add carrots, onions, garlic, and celery. While they are cooking, roll the veal shanks in flour. Push vegetables aside, and brown the veal on all sides. Add all other ingredients, cover pan, lower heat, and simmer for 1½ hours, or until meat is tender. Serves three.

PASTA CHILI

1 T oil
1 lb ground beef
½ a bell pepper, chopped (or substitute frozen, chopped bell pepper)
1 can (16 oz) tomatoes, chopped
1 can (15 oz) kidney beans, or home-cooked beans
1 can (8 oz) tomato sauce
8 oz uncooked macaroni or other pasta
1 tsp chili powder
1 tsp oregano
½ c water

Heat oil in a large skillet or pot that has a cover. Brown meat in the oil and drain off fat. Add all other ingredients and bring to a boil. Lower the heat and simmer 20 minutes. Stir several times during cooking. Serves four.

PEPPER STEAK

Serve with rice.

1 T oil
1 lb thin-sliced pepper steak
1–2 cloves garlic, minced
1 medium onion, sliced
1 bell pepper, sliced, or substitute frozen, diced bell peppers
1 T low-sodium soy sauce
1 tsp Worcestershire sauce
½ c fresh bean sprouts (optional)
4–5 fresh mushrooms, sliced (optional)

Prepare all vegetables. Heat oil in a large skillet. Add meat, garlic, and onion and stir until meat begins to brown. Add all other ingredients. Cook and stir at high heat for 5 minutes. Serves three to five.

POT ROAST

A good recipe for Passover, Chanukah, or as an everyday favorite.

1 T oil
3–4 lb beef pot roast
1 onion, sliced
½ c water
1 rib celery, sliced
1 tsp dried parsley or 1 T fresh parsley
½ tsp crushed rosemary or a sprig of fresh rosemary (optional)
dash of pepper
salt to taste (optional)
3–6 carrots, cut in chunks
3–5 small potatoes, quartered

Brown meat and onion in the oil in a heavy pan. Add all ingredients except carrots and potatoes. Cover and simmer for 3 or more hours, until meat is tender. Add vegetables, and cook ½ hour more. Serves six.

Variation: For Yankee Pot Roast, add 2 or 3 turnips or a rutabaga. Many other vegetables can be added to Pot Roast: yams, brussels sprouts, parsnips, peas, green beans, and so forth. Add just before cooking time is up, to avoid overcooking the vegetable.

SALAMI AND EGGS

Cholesterol city, here we come!

6 slices salami
3–4 eggs, beaten
1 T oil

Heat oil in a large skillet. Brown the salami on both sides. Pour in the eggs and cook, turning, until eggs are set. Serves three.

SHISH KEBAB

This makes a fun meal for an outdoor barbecue. Serve with rice and a large salad.

    2 lb lean lamb, cubed
    2 T oil (olive oil is traditional)
    1 T lemon juice
    salt and pepper
    2 bay leaves
    1 large onion, sliced
    2 tomatoes, quartered (or 1 c cherry tomatoes)
    4–6 mushrooms
    1 bell pepper, cubed
    1 small eggplant, cubed

Place meat in a bowl, and add all ingredients except eggplant. Cover and *refrigerate several hours*, to marinate. Heat broiler or barbecue. Use skewers to string meat alternately with the vegetables, including the eggplant. Broil slowly until meat is tender, turning frequently. Baste with the marinade while cooking. Serves five.

SLOPPY JOES

Sloppy Joes are what the name implies—not your company fare unless you count the times when your kids have invited their little friends for dinner. Sloppy Joes are fun to serve outdoors. Supply lots of paper napkins.

    2 T oil
    1 onion, chopped
    1 clove garlic, minced
    1 lb ground beef or ground turkey
    1½ c water
    1 can (6 oz) tomato paste
    salt and pepper to taste
    4 hamburger or steak rolls

Heat oil in a saucepan and add onion and garlic. Cook over medium heat until onion begins to brown—about 5 minutes. Add ground beef and stir until meat changes color. Drain off excess fat, if any. Stir in water, tomato paste, salt, and pepper. Bring to boil. Turn heat down to low and simmer 15 to 20 minutes. Serve on rolls. Serves four.

SPAGHETTI AND MEAT SAUCE

If you feel like making this into a fancy dish, add ¼ cup mushrooms along with the onions.

1 T oil
1 lb hamburger or ground turkey meat
½ onion, chopped
2 cloves garlic, minced
1 can (8 oz) tomato sauce
1 can (6 oz) tomato paste
1 tsp oregano
pepper
1 tsp seasoned salt
8 oz spaghetti

Brown meat in oil, and drain off excess fat. Add onion and garlic. After meat is brown, add tomato sauce and paste, plus seasonings. Lower heat and simmer, stirring occasionally. In another pot, boil spaghetti in water for 10 minutes. Drain spaghetti and serve with the sauce. Serves four.

SPANISH RICE

A friend gave me this recipe soon after my marriage (umpteen years ago), and it has remained a family favorite. Both my married children phoned me for this recipe shortly after their weddings.

1 lb ground beef
1 T oil
1 large onion, diced
1 clove of garlic, minced (optional)
½ bell pepper, diced (or use frozen, diced peppers)
1 cup rice, uncooked
1 can (8 oz) tomato sauce
2 c hot water
1 tsp chili powder
1 tsp oregano

In a large pan that has a tight-fitting cover, heat oil and brown the beef. Then, drain off any excess fat. Stir in the onion and garlic (if used), and add the bell pepper. Mix in the rice and brown a few minutes longer. Add all other ingredients, bring to boil, stir, and cover. Turn heat to low and simmer 25 minutes, or until rice is tender. Serves four.

STEAK

steaks
1 tsp meat tenderizer, if necessary
1 T oil
2 onions, diced
10 mushrooms, sliced
1–2 cloves garlic, minced

Follow the directions on the meat tenderizer, if used. Place oil in a pan, and gently cook the onion, mushrooms, and garlic. Heat a broiler or barbecue, and broil the steaks until done.

STUFFED CABBAGE WITH BRISKET

This is truly an enormous recipe, enough to feed a large family or a houseful of guests. It can be cooked earlier and heated up later on. It can also be kept, refrigerated, for more than one day. If there are leftovers, they may be frozen.

Sauce mixture:
2 T margarine
1 large onion, sliced
2 cloves garlic, minced
4 c tomato juice
1 T lemon juice
¼ c brown sugar
¼ c raisins (optional)

Meat mixture:
2 lb lean ground beef
1 small onion, chopped fine
½ c rice, uncooked
salt and pepper
2 eggs, beaten

1 small brisket
2 medium-sized cabbages
1 can (1 lb) sauerkraut

Heat the margarine in a large skillet or pot, and brown the large onion and garlic. Add the sauce ingredients and heat, but do not boil.

Mix together the meat mixture. Cut out the core of the cabbages, and put in a large pot of boiling water. The leaves will loosen. Pick out the leaves with tongs, and place on a dish towel to cool slightly. Put one tablespoon of the meat on each leaf, and fold in sides, rolling up. Grease the bottom of a large roasting pan. Cut up leftover cabbage and spread in pan. Drain sauerkraut and spread on top of cabbage. Put the brisket in the center and the cabbage rolls around the sides of the pan. Pour the sauce mixture over. Cover, and bake at 325° for 2 to 2½ hours, until meat is tender. Remove meat, and carefully slice across the grain.

SWEET AND SOUR MEATBALLS

Serve with mashed potatoes or rice.

1 lb ground beef or ground turkey
1 T oil
1 onion, diced
1–2 cloves garlic, minced
1 egg or egg substitute
¼ c matzo meal or bread crumbs
2 T lemon juice
1 T brown sugar or molasses
1 can (16 oz) tomatoes, sliced
pepper and salt to taste
½ c water

Place oil in large pan, and add onion and garlic. Cook until onions are tender. In a large bowl, mix meat, egg, and crumbs. Form into large meatballs and add to onions. Brown the meatballs. Add other ingredients and simmer 30 minutes, or until done. Serves three to four.

SWEET POTATO TZIMMES

Tzimmes is a Yiddish word, meaning to make a fuss. But this recipe is really no more trouble than making a beef stew. This recipe is suitable for Passover.

Tzimmes is the Jewish equivalent of candied sweet potatoes and can be made sweeter with the addition of 1 or 2 tablespoons of brown sugar, if desired.

If you make your tzimmes with a piece of brisket, be sure to slice it with a sharp knife, thinly, across the grain.

It may be cooked in the oven at 325°, instead of on top of the stove, or it can be made in an electric frying pan or crock pot.

To make a bigger tzimmes, increase the amount of meat and vegetables!

1 T oil
1–2 lb brisket of beef or beef stew meat

1 small onion, sliced
1 c water
4 carrots, cut in chunks
2–4 sweet potatoes or yams, sliced
2 potatoes, cut in chunks (optional)
4–6 prunes (optional)
salt and pepper, to taste
1 tsp lemon juice or wine vinegar

Brown the meat and onion in the oil. Add water, cover tightly, and simmer about 1½ hours. Add other ingredients and cook ½ hour longer, or until tender. Add more water if necessary. Serves four.

SWISS STEAK

This recipe works on the principle of throw it all in the pot and cook it.

1 T oil
1 large onion, diced
2 cloves garlic, minced (optional)
1 lb slice chuck steak
½ tsp meat tenderizer
2 T flour
3–4 carrots, peeled and sliced
2–3 potatoes, peeled and sliced (optional)
1 rib celery, sliced
optional vegetables to add: ½–1 c sliced parsnip, turnip,
    rutabaga, or yams
1 tsp Worcestershire sauce
½ tsp thyme
dash of pepper
1 can (8 oz) tomato sauce
1 c water

Put oil in large pan with a cover, or an electric frying pan, if you have one. Turn heat to medium, and add onion and garlic. While they are cooking, sprinkle meat with tenderizer and flour both sides. Move onion aside and start browning meat. Peel, slice, and add carrots and potatoes, if desired. Add celery. Turn meat over when it browns on one side. Keep adding ingredients, leaving liquids until last. When meat is brown and onions are cooked, add the tomato sauce and water. Cover pan and turn heat to simmer or low. Simmer ½ hour. Turn meat over, stir vegetables, and continue to simmer for ½ hour more, or until meat is tender. Serves three or four.

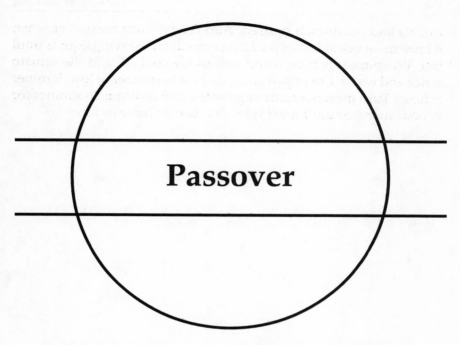

Passover

There are special dietary laws for Passover, so the recipes are limited accordingly. However, when you see all the Passover foods available in the stores, you would think that Passover lasted for a month instead of only eight days.

APPLE KUGEL (PARVE)

This is so easy to make for that big cooking day of the year, the day of the First Seder. Make the kugel in the morning and chill.

2 c matzo farfel
2 eggs, beaten
½ tsp salt
⅓ c sugar
2 T margarine or shortening
1 large cooking apple, peeled and thinly sliced
¼ c chopped nuts

Preheat oven to 350°. Grease an 8 by 8 inch pan. Place farfel in a colander or strainer, and put under the cold water tap to moisten. Drain well. Mix all ingredients together, and spread in pan. Bake ½ hour. Serve hot or cold.

BEETS AND HORSERADISH (PARVE)

This is a delicious relish for chicken or meat. Horseradish is the traditional "bitter herb" eaten on Passover.

1 horseradish, grated
2 lb beets
1 c sugar
juice of 1 lemon

Clean the beets, cover with water, and boil until tender. Allow to cool and the skins will slip off. Grate the beets, and mix with other ingredients. Add water if necessary. Chill.

CHICKEN PARTS WITH STUFFING (MEAT)

This is a favorite with children.

2 chickens, cut up
1 large onion, chopped
1 rib celery, sliced
½ c walnuts
5–6 matzos, crushed
salt and pepper
1 T minced, fresh parsley
2 tsp paprika
1 egg, beaten
1 c chicken soup
6 T oil (divided)

Saute the onion, celery, and nuts in 2 tablespoons oil, until browned. Add matzo and toast lightly. Combine with other ingredients except chicken and oil. Spread in large roasting pan. Top with chicken and brush with remaining oil. Bake at 350° for 1 hour, or until chicken is done. Serves eight.

CHORAIN (PARVE)

This is the way our family likes horseradish. Grating horseradish can cause more tears than cutting up onions. If possible, grate the horseradish outdoors. The secret to grating fresh horseradish is not to open the mouth at any time during the grating process. And keep a little towel handy! Horseradish should be soaked in water prior to grating.

1 medium horseradish, peeled and grated
1 T lemon juice
3 T juice from cooked beets (more or less)
½ tsp sugar
½ tsp salt

Mix ingredients together. Keep refrigerated in a tightly closed bottle. Keep serving dish covered with plastic until mealtime.

CRANBERRY SAUCE (PARVE)

Fresh cranberries are not in season on Passover, but there is a solution! During the Thanksgiving season, buy a package of fresh cranberries. Place the package inside a freezer bag and put in the freezer.

1 pkg cranberries
sugar
water

Cook cranberries with sugar and water according to the package directions.

FAMILY FAVORITE BORSCHT (PARVE)

Cold borscht makes a nice lunch on Passover. May be served with sliced, boiled potatoes or sour cream.

4 beets, peeled and sliced
4 c water
juice of ½ a lemon
½ tsp salt, or to taste
1 tsp sugar
½ tsp salt (optional)

Bring the beets and water to a boil, lower heat, and simmer until beets are tender. Stir in other ingredients.

FARFEL COOKED CEREAL (MILK)

This recipe may be increased according to the number of servings desired. Serve with sugar and milk.

¾ c milk
1 tsp margarine
dash of salt
½ c farfel

Heat the milk, and add the other ingredients. Cook and stir over medium heat until farfel becomes transparent. Serves one.

GRANDMA'S TZIMMES (PARVE)

Use as many vegetables it takes, according to the crowd expected.

potatoes
sweet potatoes or yams
carrots
½ c pitted prunes
½ tsp cinnamon
salt and pepper

1 tsp honey or sugar
1 T margarine
fresh parsley—for garnish

Cook vegetables with prunes in boiling water, until tender. Drain vegetables and add remaining ingredients. Serve hot, garnished with fresh parsley.

HAROSETH OR CHAROSES (PARVE)

Haroseth or, as it is often pronounced, *charoses*, is a mixture of apples and nuts eaten on Passover to remind us of the mortar used with bricks during Egyptian slavery.

This is a large recipe, enough for two nights if you hide some away from the *haroseth* lovers (like my son-in-law, Larry) at the First Seder.

Some types of apple are juicier than others, so more may be required.

4 eating apples, peeled and grated
½ c chopped walnuts
2 tsp honey (or sugar)
grated rind of one lemon (the yellow part)
2 tsp cinnamon
2–3 T sweet wine

Mix well.

LYONNAISE POTATOES (PARVE)

1 large onion, chopped
3 cooked potatoes, sliced
2 T oil
1 tsp chopped parsley
salt and pepper

Heat oil and saute the onion and potatoes until they brown. Add parsley and seasonings. Serves three or four.

MATZO BALLS

Following the dietary laws of Passover, matzo balls are Passover dumplings. The Jewish people are famous for them. Actually, people who would never dream of making a regular dumpling all year long, make matzo balls!

Matzo balls are my nephew Bram's favorites, and I have to make some for him whenever possible.

This recipe calls for chicken soup and possibly schmaltz—rendered chicken fat. If you wish to make parve matzo balls, use margarine, shortening, or oil instead of chicken fat, and substitute water, with or without parve soup powder, for the chicken soup. For the classic Chicken Soup, see the Soup chapter.

    6 T fat
    6 eggs, beaten
    1½ c matzo meal
    3 tsp salt
    dash pepper
    6 T chicken soup

Mix fat (schmaltz, margarine, shortening, or oil) with eggs. Add matzo meal and salt and pepper. Mix well. Mix in the 6 tablespoons of soup. Cover and refrigerate ½ hour or more. Bring salted water to boil in large pot. Make balls the size of walnuts. Do not overwork the dough; shape it quickly and gently. Drop the balls into the water, as they are formed. Cover and boil gently for 1 hour. *Do not lift the cover from the pot during this time.* Remove a ball, and slice it. Balls should not be grey in the middle—if they are, boil longer. Makes enough for fourteen people.

MATZO BRIE (PARVE)

This is another famous Passover recipe—sort of a Passover version of French toast. Serve with sugar, cinnamon, honey, jam, or even ketchup.

    3–4 matzos, broken
    4 eggs, beaten
    1 T oil

Place broken matzos in a colander and place under hot running water. Drain. Mix with the eggs and fry in the hot oil, turning once. Serves two or three.

ORANGE YAMS (PARVE)

4 medium yams or sweet potatoes
¼ c brown sugar, packed
2 T margarine
grated rind of one orange (the orange part)
¼ c orange juice
½ tsp salt
dash pepper

Boil yams until tender. Drain, cool slightly, and peel. Mix in remaining ingredients. Serves four to six.

PANCAKES (PARVE)

2 c matzo farfel
1 c water
2 eggs, beaten
½ tsp salt
oil

Mix ingredients except oil. Heat oil in skillet and drop batter from a large spoon. Turn once. Serve hot. Serves four.

Easy Pancake Syrup (Parve)

1 c water
1 lb brown sugar

Heat water to boiling. Lower heat and add sugar. Stir until sugar is dissolved. Best served hot. Makes 2 cups.

PASSOVER CARROT TZIMMES (MEAT)

Tzimmes is a vegetable dish, usually containing carrots.

5 beef bones
4 c water
salt and pepper
1 large onion, chopped
1 lb carrots
½ lb sweet or white potatoes
12 prunes (optional)
1 T sugar
matzo balls may be added

Cook bones in water for 1 hour, with salt, pepper, and onion. Add other ingredients and simmer 1 hour more. Serves eight to ten.

PASSOVER *KISHKA* (PARVE)

A *kishka* is a beef intestine. This recipe skips the part where you have to clean several feet of intestine and uses foil instead. *Kishka* can be compared to the Scottish dish haggis—in the trouble and ceremony involved in making and serving it (but without the Scottish bagpipes playing).

½ cup carrots, grated
1 large onion, chopped
½ c chopped celery
2 cloves garlic, minced
2 eggs, beaten
1 c margarine, melted
1 tsp salt
dash pepper
1 tsp chopped parsley
3 c matzo meal (1 lb box) or use regular matzo, crushed

Preheat oven to 350°. Mix all ingredients. Place ingredients down the center of a large piece of foil, like refrigerator cookies. Fold up the foil, and place on a cookie sheet or roaster pan. Bake for 45 minutes. Slice to serve. Serves ten.

PASSOVER POTATO LATKES (PARVE)

Good with applesauce. If it is not Passover, add 1 tsp baking powder.

5 potatoes
2 eggs, beaten
1 T matzo meal
½ tsp salt
pepper
small amount of grated onion (to taste)
fat or nonstick spray

Peel potatoes, and grate. Drain off liquid. Mix in eggs, matzo meal, onion, salt, and pepper. Drop by tablespoons on a hot pan and fry. Serves six.

PASSOVER ROLLS (PARVE)

You can't eat bread on Passover, so how about puff rolls? These can be cut open and eaten with butter, margarine, and jam; or they can be made into a dessert, by filling with cooked fruit, sliced strawberries, or a sweet filling. You might even consider making a "sandwich."

⅔ c water
⅓ c oil
1 tsp sugar
¼ tsp salt
½ c matzo meal
½ c cake meal
3 eggs

Preheat oven to 375°. Grease a cookie sheet, or spray with nonstick spray. In a large saucepan, heat water, oil, sugar, and salt to boiling. Add matzo meal and cake meal all at once, and stir over heat until mixture forms a ball. Remove from stove and let cool about 5 minutes. Beat in eggs, one at a time. Moisten hands with water, form into balls, and place on a cookie sheet, or drop from a large spoon. Bake 35 to 40 minutes, until light brown. Cool on a rack. Makes ten to twelve.

PICKLED BEETS (PARVE)

Beets used to be one of the few vegetables available in Europe during the winter and early spring, so there are a lot of traditional beet recipes for Passover time.

½ c vinegar
1 sliced onion
¼ c sugar
½ tsp salt
dash of pepper
1 lb beets, cooked, peeled and sliced
½ c liquid from the cooked beets

Clean the beets, and boil them until tender. Allow to cool, and the skins will slip off. Slice. Combine all ingredient and heat. Serve hot or cold. Serves six.

PICKLED PEPPERS (PARVE)

If Peter Piper picked a peck of pickled peppers . . .

4 medium sized green peppers
1 c Passover vinegar
¾ c honey

Seed peppers, and cut in rings. Cover with boiling water, and let stand 2 minutes. Drain, and cover with cold water, adding a few ice cubes. Let stand 5 minutes. Drain peppers and pack them into a pint-sized canning jar. Boil honey and vinegar, and pour over the peppers while hot, filling jar to within ½ inch of the top. Cover and let cool. Store in refrigerator.

POTATO KUGEL (PARVE)

A kugel is a pudding, sort of like an old-fashioned casserole.

6 potatoes
1 onion
1 carrot
¼ c matzo meal
salt and pepper to taste
2 eggs, beaten
¼ c oil

Peel and grate all vegetables. Mix all ingredients, and pour into a greased, 1½ quart baking dish. Bake at 375° for 1 hour, or until crisp on the edges. Serves six.

STRAWBERRY JAM (PARVE)

Often Passover time is also the beginning of fresh strawberry season.

2 c strawberries
2 c sugar
juice and grated rind of ½ a lemon

Place all ingredients in a pan and, stirring, bring gradually to a boil. Simmer 10 minutes, stirring occasionally. Skim any bubbles, and spread in a shallow pan to cool. Spoon into a pint jar and refrigerate.

STUFFED SWISS CHARD (MEAT)

Easier to make than stuffed cabbage, and with a different taste. This dish may be prepared ahead of time and reheated before serving. Add a bit of water if necessary.

14–16 leaves of Swiss chard, washed
1 lb ground beef
1 matzo, broken in small pieces
½ c water
1 egg, beaten
1 tsp salt
dash of pepper
1 large onion, sliced
¼ c lemon juice
1 T sugar
3 tomatoes, sliced
1 clove garlic, minced
½ c raisins (optional)

Trim the stems from the Swiss chard leaves. In a large saucepan, simmer together the tomatoes, onions, lemon juice, sugar, raisins, and garlic. Add salt and pepper. While this is cooking, in a separate container, soak matzo in water. Add the ground beef and egg to the matzos and form into meatballs. Wrap each one in a Swiss chard leaf. Place part of tomato mixture in bottom of a roasting pan. Set the meat rolls into the sauce and top with remaining sauce. Cover with foil or a cover, and bake at 350° for about 1 hour. Serve hot. Serves six.

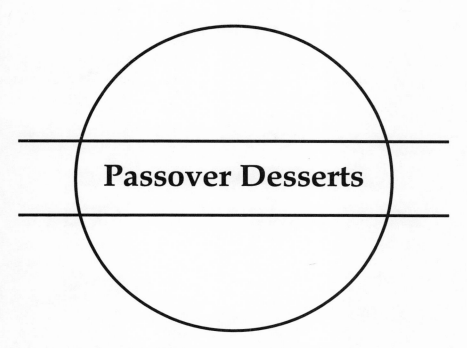

Passover Desserts

Since we don't eat leavened bread on Passover, let's eat cake!

APPLE PIE (PARVE)

If you have kids saying, "What's to eat, Mom?" or friends drop in on Passover, this easy recipe may be the answer to your problem.

4 cooking apples, peeled
¼ c water
grated rind of ½ a lemon
½ tsp cinnamon
¼ c sugar

Crust ingredients:
¼ c shortening or margarine
¼ c sugar
½ c matzo meal
dash of salt
dash of cinnamon

Thinly slice the apples and pack into a 9 inch cake pan (disposable works fine). Add the water, lemon, ½ teaspoon cinnamon, and ¼ cup sugar. In a small bowl, mix together the crust ingredients, the shortening or margarine, ¼ cup sugar, matzo meal, salt, and the dash of cinammon. Spread the mixture over the apples, and pat down lightly. Bake at 350° for ¾ hour, or until apples are tender.

COCONUT MACAROONS (PARVE)

You need a hammer and a good arm to crack a coconut. First, drive a nail into each "eye" and drain off the juice. After cracking, pry out the coconut meat with a dull knife and grate it. Kosher for Passover grated coconut may be available. You need paper muffin liners for these macaroons.

4 egg whites
6 T sugar
2 T cake meal
¹/₈ tsp salt
1½ c grated fresh coconut
1 tsp lemon juice
additional ½ c sugar

Preheat oven to 325°. Beat egg whites until stiff peaks form, gradually beating in the 6 tablespoons sugar. Fold in other ingredients. Fill paper muffin cups about ²/₃ full. Bake for 30 minutes. Makes 2 dozen.

FILLED COOKIES (PARVE)

These cookies may be filled with thick jam instead of the prune filling. They take some time to make, but they are worth it.

Dough:
½ c Passover shortening or margarine
1 c sugar
4 eggs
grated rind of ½ a lemon
2 T lemon juice
1½ c matzo meal
1 c potato starch
¹/₈ tsp salt

Cream together shortening and sugar. Beat in eggs and add lemon. Stir in other ingredients. Let stand for 1 hour to thicken. Preheat oven to 400°. Grease cookie sheets, and drop dough in mounds by tablespoonfuls. Make a dent in each cookie and fill with a teaspoonful of the filling. Bake 12 to 15 minutes. Makes 2 to 3 dozen.

Filling:
1 c dried pitted prunes
1 c dried apricots
1 lemon, seeded and sliced
¾ c sugar

Cover prunes, lemon, and apricots with a small amount of water, and simmer about 10 minutes. Stir in sugar and allow to cool. Drain fruit, and chop.

FRUIT SHERBET (PARVE)

This sherbet is refreshing, and it contains no fat. It tastes a little like pineapple. This is a Passover substitute for ice cream or sherbet.

3 bananas
3 c sugar
2 c water
1 c orange juice
juice of 3 lemons

Mash bananas well and then stir in all other ingredients. Pour into a pan approximately 9 by 12 inches. Put in the freezer. Stir every half hour for a total of three times. Cover and freeze.

HAROSETH OR *CHAROSES* CAKE (PARVE)

Haroseth is a mixture of apples and nuts eaten on Passover, to remind us of the mortar used with bricks during Egyptian slavery. This cake calls for similar ingredients. (That is, similar to *haroseth*—not mortar!)

You can use the Seven Minute Icing recipe all year around.

3 eggs
1¼ c sugar
1 c applesauce (bottled)
½ c oil
¼ c water
½ c finely chopped walnuts
1¾ c cake meal
1 tsp salt
¾ tsp baking soda
2 tsp cinnamon
¼ tsp cloves

Preheat oven to 350°. Beat eggs well, add sugar gradually, beat until thick and lemon colored. Stir in applesauce, oil, and water. Blend well. Mix dry ingredients, and add gradually, blending well. Stir in nuts. Pour into 2 greased, 8 inch round aluminum cake pans. (Disposable pans can be used.) Mixture will be thick. Bake for 30 to 35 minutes, or until done; cool in pans 10 minutes. Turn out on racks. Frost when cool.

Seven Minute Icing (Parve)

1½ c sugar
2 egg whites
5 T orange juice
1/8 tsp salt

Place all ingredients in top of a double boiler. Beat with electric beater until sugar is dissolved. Put on stove, with water boiling beneath, and beat on high speed for about 7 minutes, or until frosting will stand in peaks. Remove from heat and spread on cake.

MACAROONS (PARVE)

Macaroons are a big favorite on Passover. The recipe calls for ingredients that are easy to get, and in keeping with the special dietary laws of Passover.

4 egg whites
1 c sugar
¼ tsp salt
1 tsp lemon juice
½ c ground walnuts

Preheat oven to 250°. Grease cookie sheets. Beat egg whites until stiff. Then add sugar gradually, beating until stiff. Fold in remaining ingredients. Drop from teaspoon onto greased cookie sheet. Bake for 50 to 60 minutes and cool on racks. Makes 2 dozen.

PASSOVER DATE BARS (PARVE)

The one drawback of this recipe is that it calls for Passover baking powder—but it is so easy to make. If you can't get the baking powder at Passover, try the recipe after Passover to use up some leftover cake meal.

2 eggs, beaten
1 c sugar
¾ c cake meal
1 tsp Passover baking powder
¼ tsp salt
1 c chopped dates
1 c chopped nuts

Preheat oven to 350°. Beat eggs and add to sugar. Mix dry ingredients and nuts, then mix everything together well. Line a 7 by 11 inch pan with waxed paper and spread out the dough. Bake 30 minutes, or until done. Cut in rectangles.

PASSOVER NUT COOKIES (PARVE)

2 eggs
¾ c sugar
⅓ c oil
1 c matzo meal
1 c matzo farfel
½ tsp cinnamon
½ c raisins (or chopped dates)
½ c chopped walnuts or almonds
¼ tsp salt

Preheat oven to 350°. Beat eggs with sugar and oil. Mix in other ingredients. Drop from teaspoon onto greased cookie sheet. Bake for about 20 minutes, or until cookies brown on the bottom. Carefully transfer to racks to cool.

PASSOVER SPONGE CAKE (PARVE)

Passover is one of the few times a year when I go to the trouble of separating eggs, but this recipe is worth it.

9 eggs, separated
2 c sugar
6 T water
2 tsp grated lemon rind
½ c lemon juice
½ tsp salt   '
¾ c matzo cake meal
¾ c potato starch

Preheat oven to 325°. Beat egg yolks, very gradually adding sugar. Beat until light. Beat in water and lemon, then fold in potato starch and cake meal. Clean and dry beater well. Beat whites with salt, until they stand up in peaks. Gently fold the beaten yolks into the whites. Place into an ungreased 10 inch tube pan that comes apart. Bake for 1 hour and 15 minutes, or until done. Invert pan to cool. You may have to place the center of the pan on top of a funnel or little glass. Let the cake cool thoroughly and then cut it out of the pan.

REFRIGERATOR COOKIES FOR PASSOVER! (PARVE)

1 stick of margarine (¼ lb)
1 c sugar
2 eggs, beaten
1 c cake meal
¼ cup finely chopped almonds
1 tsp grated lemon rind
juice of 1 lemon
dash of salt

Mix the margarine with the sugar until blended. Add other ingredients, mixing well. Form into long rolls, wrapping in waxed paper. Chill *overnight* or at least several hours. Cut in slices with a sharp knife, and put on greased cookie sheet. Bake at 350° for about 15 to 20 minutes, depending upon the thickness of the cookies. Carefully transfer to racks to cool.

SYLVIA'S PASSOVER LEMON COOKIES (PARVE)

A little frosting makes a nice addition. See the Seven Minute Icing under *Haroseth* Cake.

2 eggs, separated
¼ c margarine
½ c sugar
grated rind of ½ a lemon
2 tsp lemon juice
⅔ c cake meal
¼ tsp salt
⅛ tsp baking soda

The easiest way to make this recipe is to use disposable aluminum cupcake holders. If you do not have these, grease a baking sheet or cupcake pan. Preheat oven to 350°. Measure out the ingredients before beginning to mix everything. Beat the egg whites until stiff. In another bowl, cream the margarine and sugar. Stir in the lemon rind and juice. Beat the egg yolks well and then beat them into the mixture. Add dry ingredients, and mix well. The mixture will be quite thick. Fold the beaten egg whites into the mixture. Spoon by tablespoonfuls into the muffin holders. Bake for 15 to 20 minutes, until lightly browned. Makes about 18.

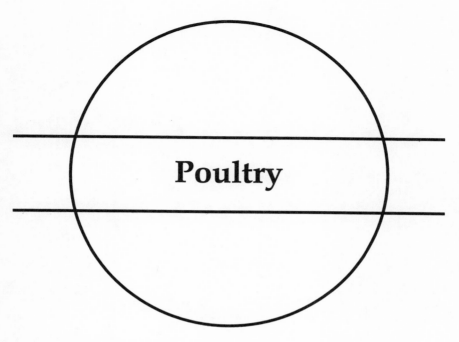

Poultry

The list of birds that are not kosher as given in the Torah (Leviticus 11:13–20) is comparable to an endangered species list—among them are the vulture, falcon, owl, and pelican. Domesticated fowl is permitted.

ADOBO—PHILIPPINE CHICKEN

Here's a different way to make chicken! The spices have a wonderful aroma.

1 chicken, cut up
2 T oil
2 cloves garlic, minced
1 T soy sauce (regular or low sodium)
3 T vinegar
1 tsp whole pickling spice
dash of pepper
½ c water

Heat oil in large pan or electric skillet, and brown chicken. This may take about 15 minutes. Drain or spoon off fat and oil from the bottom of the pan. Add all other ingredients, cover, and bring to boil. Lower heat and simmer until tender, about 35 to 45 minutes. Serves four.

ARROZ CON POLLO

This recipe is ideal for an electric skillet, but it is just as easily made in a chicken fryer on top of the stove. Served with a salad, and with a fruit for dessert, it makes a complete meal. Arroz con Pollo is Spanish for "rice with chicken."

1 chicken, cut up (or chicken parts)
2 T oil
1 onion, sliced
1 rib celery, sliced
1 clove garlic, minced
¼ of a bell pepper, sliced
1 can (16 oz) tomatoes, sliced
¾ c raw white rice
1½ c water
½ tsp basil
¼ tsp cumin
dash of pepper
1 tsp salt (optional)

Heat oil, and brown the chicken in a large skillet with a cover. Drain or spoon off fat and oil from the bottom of the pan. Add the garlic, onion, celery, and pepper, and then stir in all the other ingredients. Cover and bring to a boil. Lower the heat and simmer until tender (about 45 minutes), adding a little more hot water, if necessary. Serves four.

BARBECUED CHICKEN

The chicken is marinated, baked, and finished up on the outdoor barbecue. This sounds complicated but it is very easy, and a first-rate recipe for family or guests. If you are having a crowd, use two chickens or make some hamburgers and/or hot dogs, too.

1 chicken, cut up
1 tsp grated lemon peel
½ c lemon juice (2 lemons)
2 T oil

2 cloves garlic, minced
2–3 T chopped onion
1 tsp thyme
½ tsp salt (or to taste)
¼ tsp pepper

Place chicken in a roasting pan, and cover with ingredients. Cover and marinate in the refrigerator for several hours, turning several times. About 1 hour before the barbecue, place the pan in a 375° oven for 45 minutes. Put chicken on medium-hot grill for 15 to 20 minutes, until nicely browned, turning and basting while cooking. Serves four or five.

Variation: In case of rain, cook uncovered in a 375° oven for about 55 minutes, basting a few times.

CHICKEN À LA KING

This is *not* the version in which leftover chicken is cooked in milk! Nice served with rice.

1 T oil or margarine
1 small onion, sliced
5 sliced mushrooms or a small can of mushrooms, drained
    (optional)
2 c leftover chicken, cut up
salt and pepper to taste
½ tsp paprika
½ tsp parsley flakes or 1 T chopped fresh parsley
1 T chopped green pepper
¾ c mixed frozen vegetables
1 c water or chicken soup
2 tsp chicken-flavored bouillon or soup powder (if you are
    using the water instead of the soup)
1 T potato starch

Heat oil and brown onion, mushrooms, and chicken. Add other ingredients except potato starch. Simmer 15 minutes. Mix the potato starch with 2 tablespoons cold water, and stir into the food. Cook, stirring about 5 minutes more. Serves four.

Variations: (1) Use turkey instead of chicken. (2) Instead of paprika, substitute curry powder or cumin; add a clove of garlic, minced. (3) You can use fresh or leftover cooked vegetables instead of frozen.

CHICKEN AND BROWN RICE STEW

This recipe is easy to prepare in a covered chicken fryer or an electric skillet. It is nice to make in hot weather, when you do not want to heat up your oven.

nonstick spray
1 chicken, cut up, or about 4 lb chicken parts
1 onion, diced
1 stalk celery, sliced
3 carrots, peeled and sliced
salt and pepper to taste
1 tsp thyme
¾ c brown rice
2½ c hot water

Spray a large pan that has a well-fitting cover with nonstick spray. Brown chicken and remove from the pan. Add all other ingredients to pan, stir, and bring to a boil. Lower heat to simmer. Place chicken on top of ingredients, cover tightly, and cook for 45 minutes to 1 hour, or until rice and chicken are tender. Serves five.

Variation: (1) White rice may be substituted for brown. (2) One clove of garlic, minced; ½ teaspoon dried parsley; and/or ½ teaspoon cumin may be added for a more spicy flavor.

CHICKEN AND RICE CASSEROLE

1 chicken, cut up
1 T oil
1 rib celery, sliced
1 lemon, sliced
4 carrots, peeled and sliced
1 large onion, sliced
1 clove of garlic, minced

1 c uncooked rice
2 c hot water
1 tsp dried parsley flakes or 1 T chopped fresh parsley
salt and pepper to taste

Heat oil in a large pot that can be used in the oven, and brown the chicken. Remove any excess fat from pan. Move chicken aside, and add rice. Cover rice with chicken, then add all other ingredients. Cover and bake at 375° for 1 hour, adding extra water if necessary. Serves four.

CHICKEN BAKED IN BARBECUE SAUCE

The sauce can be used in other recipes.

1 chicken, cut up, or 2–4 chicken breasts
nonstick pan spray

The Barbecue Sauce

1 T oil
½ onion, chopped
1 rib celery, sliced
2 cloves garlic, minced
½ c ketchup
1 T vinegar
1 tsp Worcestershire sauce
1 tsp regular mustard
dash of pepper
½ c water
2 drops hot pepper sauce
salt if desired

Heat oil and brown the onion, celery, and garlic. Stir in other ingredients and simmer about 10 minutes.

To prepare the chicken: set oven to 400°. Spray a baking pan with the nonstick spray and put in the chicken, skin down. Pour the sauce over it and bake for 20 minutes. Turn chicken over, baste with the sauce, and bake 30 to 40 minutes longer, or until done. Baste with the sauce a couple of times during baking.

CHICKEN CACCIATORE

Here it is—a great Italian recipe. With a checkered tablecloth and a candle on the table, all you will be missing is the friendly Italian waiter!

2–3 lb chicken parts
1 T oil
1 onion, diced
2 T chopped frozen bell pepper (or fresh bell pepper)
1 can (16 oz) tomatoes—sliced (or can of stewed tomatoes)
1 can (8 oz) tomato sauce
2 cloves garlic, minced
pepper to taste
½ tsp oregano

Brown chicken in oil, along with onion and garlic. Remove any excess fat from pan. Add remaining ingredients and cover. Heat to boiling; then turn down heat and simmer for 1 hour, or until chicken is tender. Serve with cooked spaghetti or macaroni. Serves four.

CHICKEN LEFTOVERS AT THE CASTLE

1 T oil
1 small onion, diced
1–2 cloves garlic, minced
2 c leftover chicken, diced (approximately)
1 c leftover rice (or use instant rice) (approximately)
1 c water
1 tsp Worcestershire sauce
1 tsp soy sauce
1 tsp seasoned salt
pepper
1 c frozen mixed vegetables (or leftover vegetables)

Heat oil in a large skillet and brown the onion and garlic. Add chicken and stir. Then, add all other ingredients. Cover and simmer until vegetables are done and food is heated through. Add more water, if necessary. The number of servings varies, according to how much chicken and rice you have.

Variation: Turkey can be used instead of chicken. Also, ¼ cup mushrooms may be added to this dish.

CHICKEN SKILLET

Here's an easy recipe for times when you don't want to heat up the kitchen but need a hearty meal. If you have 1 cup chicken soup handy, substitute it for the water and soup powder.

1 chicken, cut up
2 T oil
1 onion, sliced
2 cloves garlic, minced (optional)
1 rib celery, sliced
2 large or 3 medium potatoes, sliced
2 carrots, sliced
1 tsp thyme
½ bay leaf
salt and pepper to taste
1 c water
1 tsp or 1 cube chicken-flavor bouillon powder
1 cup frozen vegetables, such as green beans or peas

In large skillet with a cover or an electric skillet, heat oil and brown the chicken, onion, and garlic. Remove any excess fat from pan. Add all ingredients except frozen vegetables. Bring to boil, reduce heat, cover, and simmer for 40 minutes, or until chicken is done. Add frozen vegetables and cook for 5 to 10 more minutes, until vegetables are done. Remove bay leaf. Serves four.

CHICKEN SUPREME

If you are using frozen chicken breasts, cut in chunks and allow slightly more cooking time. Serve with potatoes, rice, or noodles. Chicken soup can be substituted for the water and soup powder.

1 T oil
1 onion, chopped
2 garlic cloves, minced
2–3 chicken breasts
1 can (7 oz) mushrooms, drained (or use ½ c sliced fresh mushrooms)
1 T lemon juice
½ tsp salt (optional)
dash of pepper
½ tsp cumin
1 c water
1 tsp chicken-flavored soup powder

Heat oil in a large pan. Add onion and garlic, then cook over medium heat for 5 to 10 minutes. Add chicken and mushrooms and cook 10 minutes longer, turning a couple of times. Add all other ingredients. Cover and simmer 45 minutes, or until chicken is tender. Serves three to four.

HONEY ROASTED CHICKEN

You can find chili sauce in the market, near the ketchup. It also makes a spicy change from ketchup on hamburgers or fries.

1 chicken, cut up, or chicken parts
¼ c honey
¼ c chili sauce
¼ c lemon juice

Place chicken in a roasting pan. Mix other ingredients together for a sauce and pour over the chicken. Bake at 350° for 1 hour, until tender, basting the chicken a few times. Serves four.

LEMON CHICKEN

2 skinless chicken breasts
1 T oil
1 sliced onion
1 rib celery, sliced
1 clove garlic, minced
1 T soy sauce (may be the low-sodium type)
3 T lemon juice
pepper
½ c water
1 small lemon, sliced

Brown onion, celery, and garlic in oil. Add chicken. Brown lightly. Add other ingredients and simmer, covered, for 35 to 40 minutes, or until tender, turning chicken several times during cooking. Serves two.

OVEN CHICKEN EASY

This recipe saves you money over buying the prepared baking mix, and it is just as easy. Vary the taste by using different seasonings. This recipe is suitable for Passover.

1 chicken, cut in parts
about ½ c fine bread crumbs, or matzo meal
dash of pepper
¼ tsp garlic powder
½ tsp curry, paprika, or poultry seasoning
nonstick cooking spray

Set oven at 375°. Spray a large pan with the nonstick spray. Wash chicken and put the bread crumbs and seasonings in a bag. Shake the chicken parts in the bag, one at a time. Place chicken, skin side up, in the pan. Bake 1 hour, or until done. Serves four.

Variation: Cajun Flavor Chicken—to the bread crumbs, add a mixture of the following: 1 teaspoon poultry seasoning, ¼ teaspoon cayenne pepper *or* black pepper, 1 teaspoon garlic salt, and 1 teaspoon basil. For a hot Cajun flavor, add a few drops of red hot sauce (tabasco) to the chicken before baking.

OVEN LEMON CHICKEN

chicken parts (2–6 parts, depending on the number of servings
    desired)
nonstick spray
1 tsp salt (optional)
dash of pepper
1 clove garlic, minced
¼ c lemon juice
1 T Worcestershire sauce
½ tsp parsley flakes

Spray the pan and put in the chicken. Add remaining ingredients.
Bake at 350° for 1 hour, or until chicken is tender, turning and basting chicken once or twice during cooking.

POT-ROASTED CHICKEN

A very large pot is required. This is a slow method of cooking a
chicken, but the result is extremely succulent. It is also a useful recipe
when your oven is full of other things or if the weather is hot.

1 whole chicken (about 3½ lbs)
1 lemon
½ tsp thyme
½ tsp sage
¹/₈ tsp pepper
½ tsp salt (optional)
1 tsp dried parsley flakes or 1 T chopped fresh parsley
1 tsp paprika
½ c orange juice
½ c water
3–4 potatoes, sliced
4 carrots, sliced

Squeeze lemon over chicken, inside and out. Place in a large pot.
Add all other ingredients except potatoes and carrots. Bring to a boil,
lower heat to medium low, and simmer for 1 hour. Add vegetables

and cook about 1 hour longer, or until tender. Turn the chicken a few times during cooking. Serves four to six.

Variation: Other vegetables, such as parsnips, turnips, celery, onion, garlic, or green pepper, may be added in addition to, or instead of, the potatoes and carrots.

POT-ROASTED TURKEY PARTS

Have a turkey dinner without cooking a whole turkey. This recipe is suitable for Passover.

turkey legs and other parts
2 T oil
¼ c flour or matzo meal
1 onion, sliced (optional)
2 or 3 sprigs parsley (optional)
1–2 c water
1 tsp salt (optional)

Heat oil in a large pan. Coat turkey with flour, and brown in the oil along with the onion (if used). Add parsley, water, and salt, cover, and simmer for 1 to 1½ hours, or until tender.

RICE DINNER

1 c rice
1 can (16 oz) tomatoes (sliced)
1 chicken (3–4 lbs), cut up
2 c hot water
1 large onion, sliced
1 green pepper, diced (or use frozen, diced green pepper)
1 clove garlic, minced
½ tsp Worcestershire sauce
dash pepper
½ tsp oregano
¼ tsp basil or thyme
½ tsp salt (optional)

Place rice in the bottom of a large pan and add tomatoes. Top with the chicken and add all other ingredients. Cover and bake at 350° for 1 hour, or until chicken is tender. Serves four.

ROASTED CHICKEN

an approximately 4 lb chicken, whole

Place chicken on a rack in a roasting pan, breast side down. Place in a 325° oven. After 45 minutes, turn the chicken over. Continue to cook for another 1 to 1½ hours, or until drumsticks are loose to the touch and juices from the leg joint run clear when it is pierced with fork. Serves four to six.

ROASTED TURKEY

If turkey is frozen, remove from freezer and let thaw, covered, re-frigerated, for 2 to 3 days. I usually put a reminder on my calendar, "Take out turkey." A meat thermometer is strongly recommended.

1 turkey, fresh or thawed
2 T oil or margarine

If you are planning on stuffing, stuff just before roasting. Wash turkey under cold running water and stuff lightly. Sew opening closed, or close with skewer. Place, breast side up, on a rack in a roasting pan. Coat with oil or margarine. If using a meat thermometer, insert into inside of the thigh muscle.

Roast at 325°. (See guidelines below.) After 2 to 3 hours, check to see if the bird is browning. When skin is brown, take a big piece of foil. Fold it in the center lengthwise, to make a "tent." Put the foil loosely over bird for the remainder of the cooking time. A meat thermometer inserted in the thigh should register 180°. Or, check to see if the bird is done by seeing if the drumsticks are getting tender and if they can be moved up and down easily. When the inner part of the drumstick is pierced with a fork, the fluid should run clear, not pink. Remove the bird from the oven and let stand 20 to 30 minutes before carving, to allow juices to set. Remove stuffing from turkey and refrigerate separately. Refrigerate all poultry promptly.

Turkey Cooking Guidelines

Pounds weight	Unstuffed—hours	Stuffed—hours
8–12	2¾ to 3	3 to 3½
12–14	3 to 3¾	3½ to 4
14–18	3¾ to 4¼	4 to 4¼
18–20	4¼ to 4½	4¼ to 4¾
20–24	4½ to 5	4¾ to 5¼

SCHMALTZ AND *GRIBNES*

This is for those not afraid of cholesterol! It is pure fat. I used to make it for Passover in the good old days. My Cousin Lenny loves *gribnes*, but I doubt if he still eats them.

¼–2 c fat from chickens and turkeys
bit of chicken skin
1 small onion, diced
¼ c water

Use a very heavy pan. Cut up the fat and place all ingredients in the pan over low heat. As it cooks, spoon off the clear fat (the schmaltz) into a jar. The safest thing to do is to place a teaspoon into the jar to prevent it from breaking as hot fat is poured into it. The *gribnes* is the brown stuff left over in the pan. If no one in the family is around to "nosh" (snack) on the *gribnes*—and you actually have any left after the smell attracts everyone to the kitchen—add *gribnes* to the stuffing of a turkey or chicken.

Use the schmaltz as a cooking fat, for instance, in matzo balls. It is also used to flavor chopped liver, or as a spread on matzo.

TERIYAKI CHICKEN

For this recipe, you need skewers. Serve with rice. This is another recipe that makes a fun outdoor meal.

2–3 chicken breasts (boned, and skinned)
3–4 of the following vegetables:
1 onion, cut in squares, or several small, whole onions
6 cherry tomatoes
1 green pepper, cut in squares
6 mushrooms
1 zucchini, cut in chunks

Mix the following in a pan for the marinade (or use bottled teriyaki sauce):

2 T soy sauce
¼ c brown sugar
2 T oil
1 tsp ginger
½ c wine vinegar
1 clove garlic, minced
dash of hot red pepper sauce

Prepare teriyaki marinade. Cut chicken in strips and thread on skewers. Place in the marinade. Prepare the vegetables and put them in rows on the skewers. Place in marinade and cover pan. Leave the chicken and vegetables in the refrigerator to marinate for a minimum of 1 hour (up to several hours), turning once in awhile. Remove from the marinade and broil or barbecue for about 5 minutes, turning to cook on all sides. Remove the skewers and serve. Serves two to four.

Salad Dressings and Sauces

The simplest dressing for a salad is oil, vinegar, salt, and pepper.

CHARLENE'S SECRET SALAD DRESSING (PARVE)

¼ c lemon juice or vinegar
¾ c oil
⅛ tsp garlic powder
⅛ tsp pepper
½ tsp salt
¼ tsp paprika
¼ c chili sauce (next to the ketchup in the supermarket)

Mix all ingredients. Place in a jar and chill. Shake and then serve over green salad, tuna fish, or cucumbers.

COLESLAW HONEY MUSTARD DRESSING (PARVE)

⅓ c mayonnaise (regular or diet)
1 T lemon juice
1 tsp honey
1 tsp prepared mustard

Mix well and chill.

COOKED SALAD DRESSING (PARVE)

This dressing is nonfat and contains no milk.

   2 tsp potato starch
   ½ tsp dry mustard
   1¼ c water
   3 T vinegar (or to taste)
   1 tsp ketchup
   ½ tsp paprika
   ½ tsp prepared horseradish
   ½ tsp Worcestershire sauce
   ¼ tsp garlic powder
   ½ tsp salt
   ½ tsp dried parsley flakes

Mix potato starch and dry mustard in a saucepan. Gradually stir in water. Cook, stirring, over medium heat until mixture thickens. Remove from heat and stir in other ingredients. Chill.

DIET DRESSING (PARVE)

   1¼ c tomato juice
   1 T diced green pepper
   ½ tsp Worchestshire sauce
   2 tsp lemon juice or vinegar
   ½ tsp onion or celery salt
   dash of pepper

Mix and chill.

TARTAR SAUCE (PARVE)

   ½ c mayonnaise (regular or diet)
   1 T vinegar or lemon juice
   2 T pickle relish

Mix well and chill. Serve with fish.

THOUSAND ISLAND DRESSING (PARVE)

This makes a good dip for raw vegetables like carrots, celery sticks, radishes, and cucumbers.

1 c mayonnaise (regular or diet)
1/3 c ketchup
3 T sweet pickle relish

Stir together and chill.

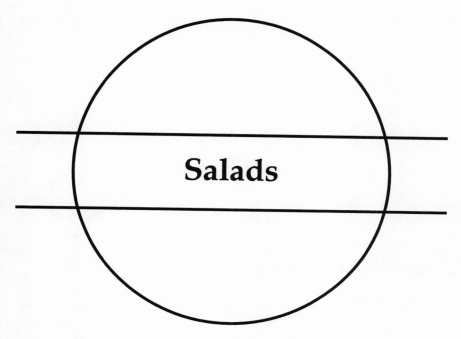

Salads

Use crisp fresh vegetables and fruits for salads. Romaine or loose-leaf lettuces provide variety and often better nutrition than the standard head lettuce.

BANQUET SALAD (PARVE)

This makes a lovely salad for a crowd. It looks very attractive in a glass bowl.

1 head lettuce
5 green onions or chives
5–10 ribs celery
2 c frozen peas, thawed
1 green pepper (optional)
1 tsp celery salt or onion salt
½ tsp garlic powder
1 c mayonnaise
4–5 sliced, hard-cooked eggs
5–6 cherry tomatoes or 1 small tomato, diced

Cut up vegetables, including lettuce, and layer, in order given, in a large bowl. Spread the mayonnaise evenly over top, and garnish with eggs and tomatoes. Toss just before serving. Serves eight to ten.

CALIFORNIA PASTA SALAD (PARVE)

You can serve this salad equally well at a picnic or a sit-down dinner. It is quick and easy to make. Pack it in a disposable pan to bring along to a party.

8 oz salad macaroni or curly pasta
¼ c green onion or chives, sliced
1 small green pepper, diced
1 large carrot, shredded
1 rib celery, diced
1 tomato, diced
2 T oil
2 T vinegar or lemon juice
½ tsp oregano
½ tsp garlic or onion salt
3–4 drops hot sauce

Cook pasta as package directs. Rinse with cold water and drain. Combine with all ingredients in a large bowl and chill. Serves eight.

CARROT SALAD (PARVE)

This salad is served at breakfast in hotels in Israel, where they serve bread, cheese, hard-cooked eggs, and salads. It is a refreshing change from our American breakfast fare. The hotel where we went also served eggs, cereal, and toast for the less adventurous. This recipe is suitable for Passover.

4 carrots, grated
¼ c raisins
¼ c orange juice
½ tsp sugar
¼ tsp salt

Mix all ingredients and chill. Serves three or four.

Variation: For an American-style salad, substitute mayonnaise for the orange juice and sugar.

CHICKPEA SALAD (PARVE)

This is a good dish to make on Friday for serving on *Shabbat*. Chickpeas have more than one name—they are also called cici beans and garbanzos.

1 can (15 oz) chickpeas, drained, or use 2 cups cooked chickpeas
½ c Italian salad dressing
3 sprigs parsley
lettuce (optional)

Mix chickpeas and salad dressing. Chill and then garnish with parsley. Serve in a bowl as a snack, or on lettuce leaves.

Variation: If desired, 2 tablespoons pickle relish, ¼ cup diced bell pepper, or 1 tablespoon diced onion may be added. Serves three to four.

COLESLAW (PARVE)

If you like a creamier coleslaw or are using a large cabbage, you may want to increase or double the dressing ingredients. This is quick to make using a food processor. And coleslaw makes a practical salad in the winter, when other salad ingredients are expensive. This recipe is suitable for Passover.

For a different flavor, see the Coleslaw Honey Mustard recipe in the Salad Dressings and Sauces chapter.

1 small cabbage, shredded
3 carrots, shredded
4 T mayonnaise (regular or diet)
2 tsp sugar
1 T lemon juice
dash of pepper

Mix the mayonnaise, sugar, lemon juice, and pepper. Mix together with the cabbage and carrots and chill. Serves eight.

Variation: Add ¼ cup chopped green pepper.

CONFETTI AND RICE SALAD (PARVE)

Vegetables may be chopped using food processor.

> 1 c cooked rice (white or brown)
> 1 carrot, grated
> ¼ bell pepper, diced
> 1 rib celery, sliced
> ½ cucumber, peeled and diced
> 1 slice of onion, chopped (optional)
> dash of pepper
> ½ tsp salt
> 1 T oil
> 1 T lemon juice or vinegar

Combine all ingredients, cover, and chill. Serves four.

CORN RELISH (PARVE)

Vegetables can be chopped in a food processor, if desired.

> 1 can (16 oz) whole corn kernels, drained
> 3 green onions, sliced (or use 2 T chopped onion)
> ½ of a bell pepper, diced
> 1 rib celery, sliced
> ½ tsp celery seed
> 3 T vinegar
> 2 T sugar (or to taste)
> 1 tsp mustard
> dash of pepper
> ½ tsp salt (optional)

Mix all ingredients. Refrigerate, covered, for at least 2 hours before serving. Stir before serving. Serves four to six.

CORN SALAD (PARVE)

10 oz pkg frozen, cut corn
2 ribs celery, diced
2 tomatoes, diced
½ green pepper, diced
½ c French dressing
lettuce
3 red onion slices

Cook corn as directed on package. Drain and cool; add celery, tomato, and green pepper. Add dressing and chill. Serve on lettuce, garnished with red onion slices. Serves four.

CUCUMBER AND YOGURT SALAD (MILK)

This goes well with baked or broiled fish. It is best if served on the same day, as after that, the yogurt will tend to separate a bit.

2 cucumbers, peeled and thinly sliced
½ onion, finely chopped
2 tsp sugar (or to taste)
salt and pepper
½ c plain, nonfat yogurt

Mix together, then cover and refrigerate until serving time. Serves four.

CUCUMBER PICKLE SALAD (PARVE)

Serve this relish with cold cuts, or at a buffet or barbecue. It is made the day before, so it is a good salad to make on a Friday in preparation for *Shabbat*.

2–3 cucumbers, peeled and thinly sliced
1 T chopped onion or 1 tsp dried onion flakes
2 tsp mixed pickling spices
¼ c vinegar
juice of ½ lemon
½ c water
dash of pepper
½ tsp sugar
½ tsp salt or celery salt
¼ tsp garlic powder

Mix all ingredients except cucumbers in a bowl; then stir in cucumber slices. Chill several hours or overnight before serving. Serves four.

CUCUMBER SALAD (PARVE)

This salad, with its simple ingredients, is ideal for Passover. Serve with cold meat or with chicken.

1 cucumber, peeled
1 small red onion or ½ of a larger one
juice of 1 small lemon (about 1 T)
¼ c water
pepper and salt to taste

Slice vegetables very thinly. Add other ingredients. Cover and chill for at least 1 hour before serving. Serves four.

Variation: Add ½ of a sweet red pepper, sliced. Also, ¼ cup Italian dressing may be used instead of the lemon and water.

FARMER'S CHOP SUEY (MILK)

This recipe is one of my mother's most delicious salads. Mom used to tell us a story about how, when she was first married, she lacked confidence in her cooking ability so she phoned her mother. Grandma's wise advice was, "Start cooking early, and keep at it until something comes out good."

Use any combination of three or more of the following vegetables, cut up:

cherry or regular tomatoes
radishes
celery
carrots
green pepper
cucumber
green onions
fresh peas

Add sour cream (or use Mock Sour Cream recipe from Appetizer section). Serve in a bowl.

FRANCINE'S CHICKPEA SALAD (PARVE)

2 c cooked or 1 can (15 oz) chickpeas, drained
½ green pepper
½ red pepper (or use 2 oz jar of canned pimiento)
2 ribs celery
½ small red onion
4–5 radishes
½ cucumber
2 T olive oil
1 T vinegar
5 drops red pepper hot sauce
salt and pepper
black olives, sliced

Chop the peppers, celery, onion, radishes, and cucumber in a food processor, or cut up small. Mix with the chickpeas, oil, vinegar, and seasonings. Garnish with the olives and serve cold. Serves four to six, or the recipe may be doubled.

GRABSIES MISSIES

This is the family version of a salad bar. It's a wonderful way to serve food on Sunday afternoon. Put out a buffet table of all the goodies and leftovers for the family. My son Seth, who named this Grabsies Missies, used to help bring out everything in the refrigerator.

For a dairy table:
cottage cheese
tuna fish
sardines
salad vegetables
bread, bagels, toast and/or crackers
cheese, cream cheese
jam
hard-boiled eggs

For a meat table use:
leftover chicken or sliced meat
cold cuts
mustard, horseradish
pickles, salsa
breads, crackers, or matzo
chips
sliced vegetables, salads

KIDNEY BEAN SALAD

This salad may be parve or dairy (if a milk-based salad dressing is used).

1 can (15 oz) kidney beans, drained (or home-cooked kidney beans)
½ bell pepper (red or green), diced
2 ribs celery, diced
1 T grated onion (optional)
1 T, or to taste, creamy salad dressing or mayonnaise

Combine all ingredients and chill. Serves two to four.

KIDNEY BEAN AND SALSA SALAD (PARVE)

1 can (15 oz) kidney beans, drained and rinsed (or home-cooked
  kidney beans)
1 can (16 oz) corn kernels (drained)
1 rib celery, chopped
1 cup Salsa (see recipe in Appetizer chapter)
2 T wine vinegar
pepper
lettuce

Combine all ingredients except lettuce, and chill. Serve on top of
lettuce. Serves three to four.

LOS ANGELES SALAD (PARVE)

This is a dependable dish to make ahead of time when expecting
company. Increase the ingredients for a crowd. This recipe is suitable for Passover.

1 large cucumber
1 tomato
½ bell pepper
½ red onion
1 rib celery
1 T lemon juice
1 T vinegar
salt and pepper to taste
¼ tsp basil

Slice all vegetables thinly or cut in small pieces. Add the other ingredients. Cover and refrigerate before serving. Serves four to six.

MACARONI SALAD (PARVE)

This is a good opportunity to get the old food processor going. If you have no food processor, a sharp knife and a cutting board are the next best thing.

8 oz small salad macaroni, or other pasta
1 c chopped cucumber
1 rib celery, diced
1 carrot, shredded
½ bell pepper, diced (optional)
1 slice onion, diced
½ c frozen peas (optional)
2 T mayonnaise (regular or diet)
1 T lemon juice
pepper and salt, to taste

Boil and drain macaroni, then add all other ingredients. Mix, cover, and chill. Serves six.

MACARONI, VEGETABLE, AND CHEESE SALAD (MILK)

8 oz macaroni
8 oz container of ricotta cheese
1 tsp prepared mustard
3 T mayonnaise
1 rib celery, sliced
1 carrot, grated
½ green pepper, diced
½ small onion, grated
½ small cucumber, diced
salt and pepper, to taste

Boil macaroni in water and drain. Allow to cool for 10 to 20 minutes. Mix in other ingredients and chill. Serves six.

Variation: For Macaroni and Tuna Salad, substitute a 6 oz can of tuna, drained, for the cheese.

MAC TUNA SALAD (FISH)

8 ounces macaroni, cooked and drained
1 can (6 oz) tuna, drained
1 small cucumber, peeled and diced
1 tomato, diced
1 rib celery, sliced
1 slice of bell pepper, chopped
1 slice onion, chopped
1 small zucchini, diced (optional)
½ c mayonnaise (regular or diet)
1 tsp salt (optional)
pepper
2 T oil
1 T lemon juice or vinegar

Rinse cooked macaroni with cold water in a colander, and drain.
Place in a bowl with all other ingredients and mix well. Cover and
chill before serving. Serves three.

MOM'S SALAD (PARVE)

This recipe is suitable for Passover.

lettuce leaves
2 small or 1 large tomato
1 cucumber, peeled
½ green pepper
French dressing

Cube the tomato and cucumber, and cut the green pepper into thin
strips. Mix with the dressing and serve on the lettuce leaves. Serves
four.

PASTA SALAD (PARVE)

8 oz pkg curly pasta spirals
16 oz pkg frozen mixed vegetables—thawed
1 rib celery, sliced
½ small onion, diced (optional)
½ c Italian salad dressing—regular or diet

Cook pasta according to package directions and drain. Mix all ingredients together, then cover and chill. Serves four.

Variation: For Pasta and Bean Salad, substitute 1 can (15 ounces) each of kidney beans and chickpeas, drained, for the frozen vegetables. Then add 1 teaspoon chopped or dried parsley.

PICKLED COLESLAW (PARVE)

This unusual salad has no fat! It is best when prepared ahead of time, and allowed to chill a few hours. It can also be served on top of salad greens. Then, no extra salad dressing would be required. It will keep for a few days in the refrigerator.

4 T vinegar
1 tsp sugar (optional)
1½ tsp mustard seed
2 tsp celery seed
¼ c dill pickle relish, or a chopped-up dill pickle
1 tsp prepared mustard
½ tsp salt
1 small cabbage (green or red), shredded

Mix vinegar, sugar, and seeds in a pan, and heat to boiling. Remove from heat, add other ingredients except cabbage, and mix well. Refrigerate dressing while chopping cabbage. Mix together, chill, and serve. Serves six to eight.

POTATO SALAD (PARVE)

I used to boil the potatoes in their skins and let them cool, then peel them and make them into salad. But I have learned that some potatoes develop green areas beneath the skin that are not good to eat, so I remove all of this first. The story that the best vitamins are nearest the skin of the potato is only an old wives' tale.

6–8 potatoes
1 rib celery, diced
1 T pickle relish
1 diced green onion or 1 slice onion, minced
1 tsp prepared mustard
½ c mayonnaise, diet or regular
pepper and salt to taste

Peel and cut up the potatoes. Put in a pot and cover with water. Bring to a boil and turn heat to simmer. Simmer 20 minutes, or until potatoes are tender when pierced with a fork—do not overcook. Drain and allow to cool. Add celery, pickle relish, and onion. Mix mustard, mayonnaise, and seasonings together. Add to potatoes. Stir together, cover, and chill. Serves five.

Variations: ⅓ cup diced bell pepper, cucumber, radishes, or 2 to 3 hard-cooked eggs may be added.

RAINBOW VALLEY SALAD

When I was driving to San Diego, California, I passed the lovely Rainbow Valley, so I named this salad after it.

Arrange any combination of the following on a large plate, the more colorful, the better:

lettuce, cut up
romaine
whole button mushrooms
red and yellow bell pepper, diced
pimientos
cherry tomatoes
small cheese squares (optional)
diced, peeled cucumbers
red cabbage, shredded
olives
radishes
alfalfa sprouts
small carrot sticks, or shredded carrots

Top with ⅓ cup croutons and ¼ cup French or Russian dressing.

SALMON SALAD (FISH)

Tuna may be used instead of salmon.

**lettuce
1 rib celery, sliced
2 tomatoes, cut up
2 c peas
1 c cooked or canned salmon
French dressing
olives**

Put lettuce on plates. Top with other ingredients, garnishing with the olives.

SIMPLE SALAD (PARVE)

This recipe is suitable for Passover.

**1 lettuce
1 tomato, cut up
½ cucumber, peeled and sliced
1–2 ribs celery, diced
¼ lemon
salt and pepper to taste**

Cut lettuce into slices. Place on a plate, cover with salad vegetables, and squeeze the lemon on top. Serves two.

SLICED TOMATOES (PARVE)

If you have a vegetable garden, this salad is a good way to serve those home-grown tomatoes. It works with cherry tomatoes, too. Just cut them in half with a sharp knife.

**1–2 large tomatoes, sliced
½ tsp basil
1 T oil
salt and pepper to taste**

Slice the tomatoes and sprinkle with basil and oil. Chill until ready to serve. Add salt and pepper, if desired.

Variation: Add 1 clove garlic, minced, or 1 tablespoon minced onion.

SPAGHETTI SALAD (MILK)

Angel hair pasta may be substituted for spaghetti.

8 oz spaghetti
1 bell pepper, diced
1 large tomato, diced (1 c canned stewed tomato may be substituted)
1 small onion, chopped
2 cloves garlic, minced (optional)
3 T oil
1 T vinegar
½ tsp salt
dash of pepper
1 tsp oregano
1 tsp basil (optional)
grated Parmesan and Romano cheese (approximately ¼ c)

Bring water for spaghetti to a boil. Break spaghetti in pieces and cook according to package directions. Drain, rinsing with cold water. Heat oil in a large skillet and add vegetables. Cook, stirring occasionally, for 10 minutes. Add salt, pepper, oregano, and basil to vegetables. Toss the cooked vegetables and spaghetti in a large bowl. Add vinegar and mix. Serve hot or allow to cool. Sprinkle with the grated cheese, then cover and chill. Serves six.

SUNSET CUCUMBER SALAD (PARVE)

This makes a picklelike salad or relish. This recipe is suitable for Passover.

  1 c vinegar
  ⅓ c cold water
  ¼ c sugar
  1 tsp salt
  1 clove garlic, minced
  dash of pepper
  2 large or 3 small cucumbers
  1 large onion

Mix all ingredients except the cucumbers and onion in a large bowl. Peel the cucumbers and onion and slice them thinly. Separate the onion into rings. Add the vegetables to the vinegar mixture and mix well. Cover and chill several hours before serving. Serves four.

THREE BEAN SALAD (PARVE)

Good to make on Friday afternoons, for noshing (snacking) on Saturdays. Home-cooked beans may be substituted for the canned.

  1 can (15 oz) kidney beans
  1 can (15 oz) chickpeas (garbanzos)
  1 can (15 oz) cut green beans
  1 small onion, diced
  3 T oil
  5 T vinegar
  1 clove garlic, minced (optional)
  ½ tsp oregano
  dash of pepper

Drain beans well. Combine all ingredients, cover, and chill. Serves six.

TUNA SALAD (FISH)

This is one of my husband's favorites. Use canned tuna either in water or oil.

1 can (6 oz) tuna, drained
¼ cup chopped celery, onion, *or* cucumber
mayonnaise or creamy salad dressing, to taste

Mix and serve on lettuce. Serves two.

WALDORF SALAD (PARVE)

This famous salad is named after the Waldorf Hotel in New York. It can be served on lettuce as an appetizer. Best when eaten the same day it is made. It is a good menu idea for Purim or for Tu B'Shevat, the New Year of the Trees.

4 apples, diced (unpeeled)
3 ribs celery
¼ c raisins (optional)
¼ c chopped walnuts
½ c mayonnaise

Mix all ingredients and chill. Serves four to six.

WILTED CABBAGE SLAW (PARVE)

1 small cabbage, shredded
boiling water
1 T lemon juice
3 T oil
2 T sugar
1 tsp salt
dash pepper
1 apple, peeled and diced
1 small (or ½ a medium) onion, chopped
1 tsp celery seed

Place cabbage in a heat-proof bowl. Add boiling water to cover. Let stand 10 minutes, then drain. Mix in other ingredients. Chill at least 2 hours before serving. Serves six to eight.

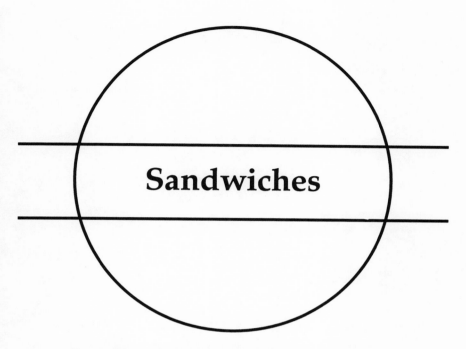

Sandwiches

As every Jewish child who has asked the Four
Questions at the Passover seder knows, the sandwich was invented not by the Earl of Sandwich
but by Hillel (born about 75 B.C.E.). He established
the rule of eating bitter herbs and *haroseth* between
two pieces of matzo (unleavened bread) at the
seder.

BAKED BEAN SANDWICH (PARVE)

4 hamburger buns
1 can vegetarian baked beans, in tomato sauce
ketchup
mustard
pickle relish (optional)

Toast the hamburger buns and heat the beans. Spread the buns with the ketchup, mustard, and pickle relish, then top with the beans. Serves four.

CALIFORNIA VEGE SANDWICH I (MILK)

pita bread
Monterey jack cheese slices or mozzarella cheese
lettuce
tomato, chopped
cucumber, peeled and chopped
radish, sliced
alfalfa sprouts
ranch dressing

Cut the end off of a pita bread round, to form a pocket. Combine all ingredients inside the bread.

CALIFORNIA VEGE SANDWICH II (MILK)

whole wheat bread
mayonnaise
lettuce
tomato slices
Monterey jack cheese slices or Edam cheese
sliced avocado
pickle slices
alfalfa sprouts

Combine ingredients between two slices of whole wheat bread.

CHICKEN SALAD SANDWICH
OR TURKEY SALAD SANDWICH (MEAT)

chopped cooked chicken or turkey
celery, chopped
sliced olives (optional)
mayonnaise
bread or rolls
lettuce and tomato slices (optional)

Mix chicken or turkey with the celery and mayonnaise. Add olives
if desired. Spread bread with the mayonnaise and the filling, add
lettuce and tomato (if used).

EGG SALAD SANDWICH (PARVE)

3 hard cooked eggs, chopped
1 rib celery, diced
mayonnaise
bread, plain or toasted
lettuce (optional)

Mix egg, celery, and moisten with mayonnaise. Spread on bread.
Serves two.

FISHWICH

1 hamburger bun for each sandwich
frozen fish fillet
Thousand Island dressing
mustard
ketchup
pickle slices
lettuce
tomato slice

Cook fish fillet as directed on package, and assemble sandwich. Excellent served with Not-Fried Fries.

Variations: A hamburger or a vegetarian burger may be substituted for the fish fillet. An onion slice may be included in the sandwich.

FRIED EGG SANDWICH (PARVE)

white toast
lettuce
tomato
ketchup
pickle slices
fried egg

Assemble and serve.

GRILLED CHEESE SANDWICH (MILK)

bread
cheese slices
butter or margarine

Put cheese between bread slices. Melt butter in a frying pan. Place sandwich in pan and cook over low heat until brown on one side. Carefully turn over, adding more butter if necessary. Brown on the other side. Serve hot.

MEAT LOAF SANDWICH

leftover meat loaf
ketchup or gravy
bread

Serve hot meat loaf, sliced, over one slice of bread, topped with hot gravy for an open-faced sandwich.

Variation: For a cold sandwich, spread bread with ketchup and top with a slice of meat loaf, and another slice of bread. Serve with pickles.

MELTED CHEESE SANDWICH (MILK)

toast
cheese slices
margarine or butter

Cover toast with butter and top with cheese. Place under broiler or in toaster oven until cheese melts.

NEW YORK DELI-STYLE SANDWICH (MEAT)

New York Deli-Style sandwiches are never made with white bread and never include mayonnaise. Serve with a pickle. Often served with coleslaw or potato salad.

rye or pumpernickel bread
mustard
cold, thin-sliced roast beef, pastrami, corned beef, salami, or
**   bologna**

TUNA SALAD SANDWICH (FISH)

**1 can (6 oz) tuna, drained
1 rib celery, diced
mayonnaise (to taste)
bread or roll
mustard (optional)
lettuce (optional)
tomato, sliced**

Mix flaked tuna with celery and mayonnaise. Serve on plain or toasted bread.

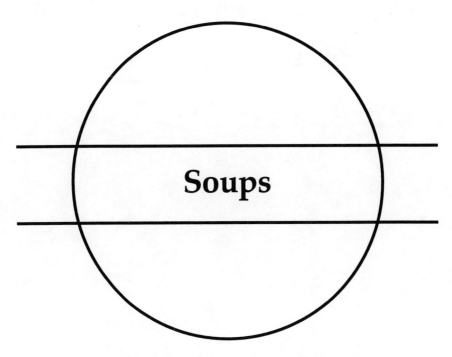

Soups

The fat in soups will rise to the top. If you want to remove the fat, chill the soup. The fat will cake on the top. Before reheating chilled soup, lift off the fat and throw it in the garbage. Never put fat down the sink, as it clogs the drains.

ABBA'S SOUP (PARVE)

(Abba means Daddy in Hebrew.)

Two good qualities of lentils and split peas is that they are very nutritious and require no presoaking like dried beans do.

2 c lentils, washed
6–8 c water
1 large onion, chopped
1 can (8 oz) tomato sauce
2 carrots, sliced
1 rib celery, sliced
½ c green beans, fresh or frozen
1 clove garlic, minced
1 potato, diced
salt and pepper to taste
½ tsp thyme

Put all ingredients in a large pot, bring to a boil. Lower heat, and simmer for 1 hour, stirring occasionally. Add more water if necessary. Serves six to eight.

BOK CHOI SOUP (PARVE)

Bok choi is a green, leafy vegetable, which is very nourishing and delicious. It is often served in Oriental dishes. Both the leaves and stalks are used. If bok choi is not available in your market, Swiss chard or spinach may be substituted.

> 2 T oil
> 2 cloves garlic, minced
> 1 large onion, diced
> 1 turnip
> 3 carrots
> 1 potato
> ½ tomato or 3–5 cherry tomatoes
> ½ bell pepper
> 2 large leaves bok choi (Swiss chard or spinach may be
>   substituted)
> ½–1 c lentils, washed
> 1 tsp salt (or to taste)
> 1 tsp seasoned salt
> dash of pepper
> 2 tsp vegetable soup powder or 2 bouillon cubes
> 6–8 c water
> ½ c macaroni

Heat oil, and cook garlic and onion for 5 minutes. Cut up all the vegetables and add along with other ingredients, except for the macaroni. Bring to a boil, lower the heat, and simmer, covered, for 50 minutes, stirring occasionally. Add the macaroni and cook 10 minutes longer. Serves six to eight (more or less vegetables may be added, according to how many servings are required).

CABBAGE BORSCHT WITH MEAT (MEAT)

Besides the popular borscht made with beets, there is also borscht made with cabbage.

> 1 lb soup meat
> 1 onion, sliced

1 can (16 oz) tomatoes, sliced
3 c water
1 small cabbage (or ½ large), shredded
¼ c raisins
salt and pepper
1 tsp sugar (or to taste)
1 T lemon juice

In a large soup pot, bring water to boil. Add meat, onion, and tomatoes, and cover. Lower heat and simmer for 2 hours. Stir in cabbage and raisins. Cook 20 minutes longer. Add salt, pepper, sugar, and lemon juice, and stir. Serve hot. Serves four.

CABBAGE SOUP (PARVE)

1 large onion, diced
1 clove garlic, minced
2 T oil
1 tsp basil
½ tsp oregano
pepper and salt
1 can (14½ oz) stewed tomatoes
½ large, or 1 small, cabbage, shredded
1 tsp vegetable soup powder or 1 bouillon cube
2 c water
½ bell pepper, diced (or use ¼ c frozen diced green pepper)
1 potato, peeled and diced (optional)
1 tsp celery seed (optional)

Put oil in a large pan and heat. Add the onion and garlic. Stir and cook until onion is limp. Add all other ingredients. Bring to a boil. Simmer 20 to 30 minutes, adding more water if necessary. Serves four.

CHICKEN AND POTATO SOUP (MEAT)

I guess there is no right or wrong way to make chicken soup—
everyone has his or her own recipe.

    1 small chicken, either whole or cut up
    1 medium onion, diced
    2–3 carrots, sliced
    3 medium potatoes, diced
    2–3 cloves garlic, minced
    ½ bay leaf
    2 sprigs parsley, diced, or 1 tsp dried parsley flakes
    ½ tsp rosemary
    salt and pepper to taste
    water
    1–2 small zucchini, diced
    4–5 sliced mushrooms
    ½ c noodles, or use Matzo Balls (optional)

Put everything but the zucchini, mushrooms, and noodles or Matzo
Balls in a big pot. Add water to cover. Cover pot, bring to boil, and
lower heat to simmer for about 1½ hours, or until chicken is very
tender. Skim off any fat. Add other ingredients, and cook 20 minutes longer. Serves five.

CHICKEN SOUP (MEAT)

This is the classic chicken soup, which is made on Passover and
holidays. If it is not Passover, ¼ to ½ cup noodles or soup alphabets
may be added in the last 15 minutes of cooking. Rice or mixed vegetables may also be added, if desired.

    1 chicken, cut up (about 4 lb)
    3 quarts water
    1 onion, diced
    3 carrots, sliced
    2 parsnips, sliced
    2 ribs celery, sliced
    3 sprigs parsley, cut up
    2 tsp salt
    dash of pepper

Cover chicken with water, and bring to a boil. Lower heat and add other ingredients. Simmer for 2 hours. Check seasoning, and add salt and pepper to taste. Serves six.

Matzo Balls

4 T shortening or rendered chicken fat (schmaltz)
4 eggs, beaten
1 c matzo meal
2 tsp salt
4 T soup or warm water

Mix shortening and eggs. Mix in matzo meal and salt, then stir in soup. Cover and then chill for ½ hour or more. Boil some salted water in a large pot that has a tight-fitting cover. Reduce heat. Form dough quickly into balls, about the size of a walnut. Do not overhandle the dough. Drop balls into the boiling water. Cover the pot tightly, and boil for 40 to 60 minutes. Do not peek while the matzo balls are cooking! Remove a matzo ball, and cut in half to see if they are done. The matzo ball should be the same color all the way through. If the center is a little darker, cover the pot and cook for about 10 more minutes.

CORN CHOWDER (MILK)

This recipe is one of my mother's best, and it made a quick lunch for us kids when we trudged home from school for lunch time (especially in the snow).

If possible, avoid boiling the milk as this may destroy some of the vitamin content.

1 T margarine or butter
1 small onion, diced
¾ c water
1 potato, peeled and diced
1 can (16 oz) cream-style corn
2 c nonfat or regular milk
dash of pepper
dash of celery salt

Melt margarine in pan and add onion. Cook until onion starts to
brown. Add potato and water to onions. Heat to boiling. Turn heat
to low, cover pot, and cook 15 minutes, or until potato is tender. Add
remaining ingredients. Canned or powdered milk may be substituted for the nonfat milk. Turn heat to medium and heat only until
hot enough to serve—do not boil. Serves four.

CREAM OF POTATO SOUP (MILK)

This recipe is suitable for Passover.

1 onion, diced
1½ T margarine or butter
1 carrot, peeled and grated
1 rib celery, sliced
3 potatoes, peeled and diced
3½ c water
salt and pepper to taste
½ tsp dried or 1 T chopped fresh parsley
1 can (12 oz) evaporated skim (nonfat) milk

Brown onion and celery in margarine. Add all ingredients except
milk. Bring to a boil, turn down heat, and simmer for 20 to 30 minutes, or until potatoes are tender. Add milk and stir—do not boil.
Serves four.

CREAM OF TUNA SOUP (MILK)

Here's a quick dish if unexpected guests arrive. Serve with crackers
or toast.

1 T oil
1 small onion, diced
1 can (6 oz) tuna, drained
1 can (16 oz) creamed-style corn
1 can (14½ oz) stewed tomatoes
dash of pepper

½ tsp basil
¼ tsp tarragon
1 c water
1 c milk (regular or nonfat)

Heat oil and add the onion. Cook over medium heat until onion starts to brown. Add all ingredients except milk. Heat to boiling. Turn down heat and simmer for 10 minutes. Stir in milk, then warm, but do not boil. Serves four to five.

CURRIED LENTIL SOUP (PARVE)

1 or 2 T oil
1 medium onion, sliced
1 clove garlic, minced
1–2 carrots, sliced
2 ribs celery, sliced
1 c lentils, washed
¼ c raw brown rice (white rice may be substituted)
¼ c frozen mixed vegetables
¼ c uncooked fine noodles
dash of pepper
½ tsp thyme
½ tsp curry powder (or to taste)
1 tsp salt

Heat oil in a pot and add onion and garlic. Cook, stirring, until onion starts to brown. Add carrots and celery, and cook, stirring for 5 more minutes. Add lentils and rice, and cover with water. Bring to a boil, then lower heat, cover pot, and simmer for 1 hour, stirring occasionally. Add remaining ingredients and more water, if necessary. Simmer 10 minutes more. Serves six to eight.

GAZPACHO (PARVE)

This is a change from the hearty soups in this chapter, as it is a cold soup.

    1 can (46 oz) tomato juice
    ½ small onion, chopped
    ½ small cucumber, chopped
    ½ green pepper, chopped
    1–2 cloves garlic, minced
    salt and pepper to taste
    2–4 drops of red hot sauce
    1 tsp olive oil
    1 tsp lemon juice
    croutons or diced toast (optional)

Mix all ingredients except croutons and chill. Shake or stir before serving, then add croutons. Serves four.

GREAT NORTHERN SOUP (PARVE)

If great northern beans are not available, use some other small dried bean.

    ¾ c dried great northern beans (washed)
    ¼ c barley
    1 rib celery, sliced
    1–2 carrots, sliced
    1 onion, sliced
    1 parsnip, sliced
    ¼ c frozen soy beans (optional)
    1 tsp salt
    dash of pepper
    ½ tsp garlic powder

Cover beans with water and bring to boil. Boil 3 minutes. Turn off heat, and let beans stand to soak for 1 hour. Add all ingredients except salt, pepper, and garlic powder. Add more water, if necessary, and then bring to a boil. Lower heat and simmer 1 hour, or until beans are tender. Add remaining ingredients. This should be a rather thick soup. Serves six.

LENTIL SOUP

It was for lentil soup that Esau traded his birthright with Jacob. This recipe may be doubled. It is parve unless you decide to add hot dogs.

1 c lentils, washed
1 small onion, diced
1 T oil
1 clove garlic, minced
1 carrot, sliced
1 rib celery, sliced
1 small potato, diced
½ tsp salt
dash of pepper
5 cups water
1 tsp dried parsley flakes or 1 T chopped fresh parsley

Heat oil and add onion and garlic, cook until browned on the edges. Add all other ingredients, bring to a boil. Lower heat and simmer 45 minutes. Serves four to six.

Variation: Add 2 or 3 sliced hot dogs the last 15 minutes of cooking time.

LENTIL VEGETABLE SOUP (PARVE)

2 c lentils, washed
1 can (16 oz) tomatoes, chopped
2 carrots, peeled and sliced
1 leek, cleaned and sliced
2 cloves garlic, minced
½ tsp basil
4–5 fresh mushrooms, sliced (or small can (7 oz) of mushrooms)
½ tsp rosemary
dash of pepper
½ tsp salt (or to taste)
8 c water

Place all ingredients in a large soup pot. Cover and bring to a boil. Turn down heat to low and simmer 1 hour. Stir occasionally. Serves six.

MEATLESS GREEN PEA SOUP (PARVE)

The vegetables for this soup can be chopped in a food processor. This recipe makes a large amount of soup. If you are warming it up the next day, add a little water and stir frequently over low heat. It is easier to warm it up in the oven, covered, at low heat.

8 c water
3 carrots, grated or sliced
1 c dried green split peas
2 ribs celery, diced
1 small onion, diced
1 small potato, diced
¼ tsp marjoram
½ tsp thyme
salt and pepper to taste
¼ c soup alphabets or noodles (optional)

Place all ingredients except alphabets in a large pot. Cover and bring to a boil. Turn down heat and simmer 1 hour. Add alphabets, if used, last 15 minutes of cooking. Stir occasionally while cooking. Add more water if necessary. Serves six to eight.

Variations: Substitute 1 teaspoon cumin for the marjoram and thyme. ½ cup lentils may be substituted for half the split peas. Yellow split peas may be used instead of green.

MINESTRONE SOUP (PARVE)

One-half cup cooked chickpeas may be added to the minestrone soup.

1 T oil
1 onion, chopped
1 clove garlic, minced

1 rib celery, diced
¼ c chopped bell pepper
1 small zucchini, diced
1 large tomato, diced
1 tsp parsley flakes (or 1 T chopped fresh parsley)
½ tsp thyme
2 tsp soup powder, or 2 bouillon cubes
½ tsp salt
dash of pepper
4 c water
½ c macaroni, broken spaghetti, or thin noodles

Heat oil in a large pot and add vegetables. Cook over medium heat, stirring, for about 10 minutes. Add remaining ingredients except macaroni, cover, and bring to boil. Lower heat, cover, and simmer for 20 minutes. Stir in macaroni and cook 15 minutes more. Serves five.

MUSHROOM BARLEY SOUP (PARVE)

1 T margarine or butter
1 medium onion, diced
1 c sliced mushrooms (5 or 6 mushrooms)
2 carrots, sliced
1–2 parsnips, sliced
1 c barley
salt and pepper to taste
1 tsp dried or 1 T chopped fresh parsley
6 c water
2 vegetable bouillon cubes or 1 T soup powder

Melt margarine in large pot, and cook onions and mushrooms over medium low heat for about 10 minutes. Add all ingredients and bring to a boil. Simmer 1 hour, or until barley is tender. Serves six.

NEW TRAIN SOUP (PARVE)

2 T oil
1 medium onion, diced
1 clove garlic, minced
3 carrots, sliced
¼ c dried beans (such as baby limas or great northern)
6 c water
1 potato, diced
¼ of a red cabbage, chopped
¼ c chopped bell pepper
1 tsp Worcestershire sauce
salt and pepper to taste
½ tsp thyme
½ c noodles
½ c frozen mixed vegetables

Soak beans by placing them in boiling water. Boil for 5 minutes. Let stand in the water for 1 hour. In a large pot, cook onion, garlic, and carrot in the oil until onion starts to brown. Add all other ingredients except noodles and frozen vegetables. Bring to boil, lower heat, and simmer 1 to 2 hours, or until beans are tender. Add noodles and frozen vegetables, and bring to a boil. Simmer for 15 minutes longer. Add more hot water to the soup during cooking if necessary. Serves six.

NOTHING SOUP (MEAT)

Made out of "nothing" but a few dribs and drabs, this nourishing soup will hit the spot during cold or rainy weather. Feel free to add any good leftovers you can find. I have even put leftover spaghetti and meat sauce in it.

French cooks call such a soup pot au feu.

soup bones
12 c water
2 T uncooked rice
2 T uncooked barley

2–3 ribs of celery, diced
1 T chopped parsley or 1 tsp dried parsley flakes
½ c frozen mixed vegetables
1 can (16 oz) tomatoes
1 large onion, diced
3–4 carrots, sliced
½ tsp thyme
1 tsp marjoram
salt and pepper to taste
1 tsp Worcestershire sauce
1 potato, diced

Put bones and water in a large pot and bring to a boil. Lower heat to a simmer. Add all ingredients and simmer 2 hours. Serves five.

PEA SOUP WITH MEAT (MEAT)

1 lb soup meat
soup bone
8 c water
2 tsp salt
1 c dried split peas
¼ c barley
1 medium onion, chopped
2 carrots, grated
¼ tsp marjoram
¼ tsp thyme
dash of pepper
¼ c noodles or soup alphabets

Cover meat and bone with water and bring to boil. Add all ingredients except noodles and turn heat down to simmer. Cover and cook 1 hour, or until meat is tender. Add noodles and cook 10 minutes more. Serves six.

POTATO AND ONION CHOWDER (MILK)

This is a dairy soup. Serve with croutons, toast, crackers or matzo. It is possible to make this recipe on Passover if you have the Passover ketchup.

1 T oil
1 large onion, diced
1 clove garlic, minced
4 c water
2 T ketchup
2 potatoes, diced
1 carrot, diced
1 rib celery, diced
½ green pepper, diced
2 sprigs parsley, chopped, or use 1 tsp dried parsley
1 tsp salt
dash of pepper
1 c milk (may be nonfat or skim)

Heat oil, and brown onion and garlic. Add all ingredients except milk. Heat to boiling. Turn heat low, and simmer 20 minutes, or until vegetables are tender. Turn off heat and stir in milk. Serves six.

POTATO LEEK SOUP (MILK)

2 T margarine
1 leek, sliced
3–4 potatoes, diced
1 tsp celery salt
1 tsp parsley flakes
dash of pepper
1 tsp Worcestershire sauce
4 c water
1 can (12 oz) evaporated skim milk

Cut up the leek, using the white end and the lower part of the green. Wash thoroughly. Heat margarine and cook the leek for 5 to 10 minutes over medium heat. Add all ingredients except the milk.

Heat to boiling, lower heat, cover, and simmer for 30 minutes, or until potato is tender. Stir in the milk. Do not boil. Serves six.

QUICK VEGETABLE SOUP (PARVE)

This recipe is so handy when surprise guests drop in and stay for supper.

½ c green beans (fresh or frozen)
½ c peas (fresh or frozen)
1 small onion, diced
1 large or 2 small carrots, sliced
2 potatoes, diced
1 small tomato, diced
6 c water
4 bouillon cubes or 4 tsp soup powder
1 tsp salt (or more, to taste)
dash of pepper
½ tsp marjoram
½ c noodles or soup alphabets

Place all ingredients except noodles in a large pot. Bring to boil, cover, turn down heat, and simmer 20 minutes. Add noodles and simmer for 10 more minutes. Serves six to eight.

RICE SOUP (MILK)

1 T oil
1 small onion, sliced
1 clove garlic, minced
1 rib celery, sliced
1 can (8 oz) tomato sauce
½ c raw white rice
2 c water
1 tsp oregano
½ tsp basil
pepper and salt to taste
3 T soup alphabets or broken spaghetti
1 can (12 oz) evaporated skim (nonfat) milk

Heat oil in a Dutch oven or large pot. Add onion, garlic, and celery. Cook until onion is limp. Add all ingredients except milk and soup alphabets. Mix well, cover, and bring to a boil. Turn heat down, and simmer for 15 minutes. Stir. Add soup alphabets and cook over low heat for 10 more minutes, or until rice is tender. Turn off heat and stir in the milk. Serves four to six.

SPLIT PEA AND SALAMI SOUP (MEAT)

1 medium onion
2 carrots
2 parsnips
1 rib celery
½ c cubed salami
1 T oil
½ c split peas
½ tsp salt
dash of pepper
5 c water
½ c thin noodles

Peel and dice the vegetables. Heat the oil, and add the salami and diced onion, carrots, parsnips, and celery. Cook, stirring occasionally, over medium heat until browned, about 20 minutes. Add split peas, salt, pepper, and water. Bring to boil, lower heat, and simmer for 1 hour. Add noodles and cook 10 or 15 minutes more. Serves five.

SUCCOTASH SOUP (MILK)

My husband, Ira, uses the word *succotash* to describe foods he doesn't like, so I have never told him the real name of this soup. Frozen lima beans may be used instead of the dried ones.

1 T margarine, or butter
2 T minced onion
1 carrot, sliced
1 rib celery, sliced

1 can (15 oz) butter or lima beans, or use 2 c home-cooked
　　lima beans
1 can (16 oz) cream-style corn
salt and pepper to taste
1 tsp sugar
2 c water
1 can (12 oz) evaporated skim milk

Cook onion, celery, and carrot in the margarine, until lightly
browned. Add all ingredients except milk. Bring to boil. Turn heat
down, and simmer for 30 minutes. Add milk right before serving.
Serves four.

SURPRISE SOUP (MEAT)

The surprise comes from the hot dogs in this soup.

1 T olive oil
2 cloves garlic, minced
1 large onion, diced
½ green pepper, diced
3 hot dogs, sliced
1½ c chickpeas, cooked or canned (drained)
1 potato, diced
5 c water
salt and pepper
3 tsp beef-flavor soup powder, or bouillon cubes

Saute the garlic, onion, green pepper, and hot dogs in the oil over
medium heat, until onion starts to brown. Add all ingredients and
bring to boil. Lower heat and simmer about 40 minutes. Serves six.

TOMATO BEAN SOUP (PARVE)

Butter bean is another name for lima bean. You can use 2 cup home-cooked beans instead of the canned—just add ½ to 1 cup of the water from the bean cooking to the soup.

1 can (15 oz) vegetarian butter beans, undrained
1 can (14½ oz) stewed tomatoes
1 T margarine
1 clove garlic, minced (optional)
½ small onion, diced
1 celery stalk, diced
pepper

Melt margarine and add onion, celery, and garlic. Brown the vegetables. Add other ingredients and simmer 20 minutes. Serves four.

TOMATO HE-MAN SOUP (MEAT)

Many recipes tell you to skim soup. I used to, but I never do it anymore and it doesn't seem to make a difference.

Soup with marrow bones is very nourishing. If you have a house full of sick kids, make chicken soup. When they finish the chicken soup, try some of this. To your good health!

soup bones
water
1 small onion, diced
1 carrot, sliced
1 rib celery, sliced
3 fresh mushrooms, sliced
1 can (8 oz) tomato sauce
pepper and salt, to taste
1 tsp oregano
¼ c frozen mixed vegetables
2 T pearl barley
2 T rice
1 T soup alphabets or broken spaghetti

Cover soup bones with water. Bring to a boil. Add onion, lower heat, and simmer 1 hour. Add all ingredients except the soup alphabets. Simmer for another hour. Add alphabets and cook for 20 minutes more. Serves six.

TURKEY BONE SOUP (MEAT)

Use up the leftover turkey bones, turkey neck, and vegetables from a big dinner to make a nourishing and economical soup. Just remember to refrigerate the turkey leftovers promptly after serving the turkey.

  bones from roast turkey
  water to cover
  1 tsp salt (or to taste)
  pepper
  ¼ tsp marjoram
  ½ tsp thyme
  1 celery stalk, sliced
  2 carrots, sliced
  2–3 parsnips, sliced
  1 tsp parsley flakes, or 1 T chopped fresh parsley
  1 small onion, sliced

Put all in a big pot. Heat to boiling, lower heat, cover, and simmer for about 2 hours, or until meat falls from bones. Serve hot. Serves four to six.

Variation: Add ½ cup rice, ½ cup leftover or frozen vegetables, 2 tablespoons soup alphabets, Dumplings, Matzo Balls, or ¼ to ½ cup noodles.

VEGETABLE BARLEY SOUP (PARVE)

A food processor makes quick work of grating the vegetables. Other vegetables may be added, if desired.

2 T barley
6 c water
2 tsp soup powder
1 potato, grated
1 onion, grated
2 carrots, grated
2 T diced green pepper
2 mushrooms, sliced
pepper and salt to taste
2 T soup alphabets

Bring water and barley to boil, then add soup powder. Chop up the vegetables and add all ingredients. Simmer 30 minutes, or until barley is tender. Serves four.

VEGETABLE BEAN SOUP (PARVE)

¼ c dried beans (baby limas or great northern)
¼ c brown rice or barley
1 can (8 oz) tomato sauce
1 diced onion
1 diced potato
1 rib celery, sliced
2–3 carrots, sliced
2–3 parsnips, sliced
2–3 fresh mushrooms, sliced
½ c frozen mixed vegetables
salt and pepper to taste
1 tsp dried parsley flakes or 1 T chopped fresh parsley
½ tsp thyme
1 clove garlic, minced
½ c uncooked macaroni, soup alphabets, or noodles

Wash dry beans and place in a large pot with 4 cups water. Bring to a boil and boil for 5 minutes. Turn off heat, and let sit 1 hour. Add 8 more cups water and the other ingredients except the macaroni. Bring to boil, lower heat, and simmer 1 hour, or until beans are tender. Add macaroni and cook 15 minutes more. Serves eight.

VEGETABLE BEEF SOUP (MEAT)

14 c water
½ c dried small white beans
1 onion, sliced
1 lb soup meat
2 carrots, sliced
1 parsnip, sliced
2 ribs celery, sliced
2 T barley
¼ c rice
½ c dried split peas or lentils
1 can (8 oz) tomato sauce
1 T salt (or to taste)
dash pepper
½ c broken spaghetti or noodles
1 c frozen mixed vegetables

In a large pot bring water to a boil, adding beans, meat, and onion. Lower heat and simmer for 1 hour. Add carrots, parsnip, celery, barley, rice, split peas, and tomato sauce. Cook 1 hour longer. Add salt, pepper, spaghetti, and frozen vegetables. Cook 15 minutes more. Serves eight.

YAM YAM SOUP (MILK)

A yam and a sweet potato are two entirely different vegetables, but they may be used interchangeably in recipes.

If you have a food processor, chop the onion first and start cooking it while you process the other vegetables. It makes quick work of preparing this nutritious soup.

1 T oil
1 large onion, chopped
2 carrots, grated
1 medium yam, peeled and cut in cubes
1 rib celery, sliced
5 c water
1 tsp salt
dash of pepper
½ tsp tarragon
½ c milk, regular or nonfat

Heat oil in a large pot. Brown the onion in the oil. Stir in the other ingredients except the milk. Bring to a boil, lower heat, and simmer for 45 minutes. Turn off heat and stir in milk. Serves six.

Fresh Vegetables: From Artichoke to Zucchini

A Vegetable Preparation Dictionary

While many vegetables are eaten raw, there are also numerous ways to cook them. This little vegetable dictionary lists the most common vegetables and gives the basics for preparing each. This is not an encyclopedia, I am sure I have not included *every* vegetable here. And some vegetables are not available in every part of the country. New vegetables are developed or forgotten ones rediscovered from time to time. Some are the favorites of different ethnic groups.

While it is true that popular vegetables like celery and potatoes are available in our stores all year around, some vegetables are seasonal and thus are cheaper and more abundant at certain times. Watch the advertisements for fresh vegetables, and find those that are freshest and most reasonably priced in the stores.

HOW TO STEAM VEGETABLES

There are several kinds of vegetable steamers. One type is an inexpensive, expandable basket insert for almost any pot. The water is put under the insert, and the vegetables are placed in the basket. The pot is covered, and vegetables are cooked until tender when pierced with a fork.

Then, there are pots you can buy that come in two parts. The bottom half is for the water, and the vegetables are placed in a perforated top portion.

The idea behind a steamer is that the vegetables are cooked quickly and without water, in order to preserve taste and nutrients. Vegetables that are steamed properly are crispy, tender, and tasty. Steaming is also a quick and easy way to cook vegetables. If you wish to cook more than one vegetable at a time, you may want to put slower-cooking ones (like carrots, for instance) in first.

Pour water into the steamer to a depth of about 2 inches. Place the vegetables in the basket or steamer top, cover pan, and turn heat to high.

Save the liquid from steaming or boiling vegetables and use as a base in soups, instead of using plain water. Water from boiled potatoes is especially good for use in making yeast breads.

ARTICHOKE

The artichoke is a perennial vegetable that produces a beautiful blue flower. It is the flower bud that we eat. Watch out for the sharp points on the ends of the petals.

How to cook a fresh artichoke: Trim off the very end of the stem, and some of the sharp points, if necessary. Place in a pot and cover with water. Cover the pot and bring to a boil. Turn the heat down, and simmer about 20 minutes, depending upon the size of the artichoke. The choke is done when you can stick a fork easily into the stem.

To eat, peel off each leaf and dip it in some mayonnaise or melted butter, if desired. Chew off the soft end of the petal. Discard the rest of the petal. Continue to eat each petal end until you reach the artichoke heart. This tender part is the big treat in each artichoke. Cut in half and remove the strings from the center.

Artichoke hearts are available in little bottles, pickled. The pickled artichoke hearts make a good addition to salad, or may be used as a garnish.

ASPARAGUS

This vegetable luxury appears in the stores in spring, when the asparagus tips push their way up to the sun. The best way to prepare asparagus is to steam it. You may need to trim off the tough bottom end of each asparagus spear. If you wish to cook the asparagus without cutting up each spear, place in a large pan with a little water, cover and cook only until the asparagus becomes tender, and changes color. Try not to overcook this delicate vegetable. Left over asparagus (if you have such a thing in your house) can be used in soups or casseroles.

BEANS

Trim the stem end from fresh beans. Green beans or wax beans may be steamed or boiled. Test with a fork to see when the beans are tender. Fresh lima beans should be boiled for about 15 minutes, or until tender.

BEANS, DRIED

Store dried beans in a bottle. Dried beans should be cleaned before using. Check for dirt and then wash in a colander. It is not always necessary to soak beans before cooking; sometimes, beans can just be cooked for a longer time. To soak dried beans, cover with water, and leave overnight. I usually place them in the refrigerator, to prevent souring. The quick way to soak beans is the method usually recommended in recipes in this book: cover with water, bring to boil, and simmer for 3 to 5 minutes. Turn off heat and let beans stand, covered, for 1 hour. Then, proceed with the cooking.

BEETS

Cut off the tops about 1 inch from the beets. (If the top leaves are nice, they can be cooked in boiling water and served as a cooked vegetable.) Scrub the beets with a brush, cover with water, and boil until tender, about 30 minutes, according to the size of the beets. Allow to cool, and take off the skin and tops by rubbing them. Serve the beets whole or sliced.

BROCCOLI

Trim off the very bottom of the stem. Cut off the rest of the stem and slice it lengthwise, to speed cooking time. Cut the top of the broccoli into "trees." Steam about 5 to 12 minutes, depending on the amount of broccoli.

BRUSSELS SPROUTS

Trim off the very bottom of the stems. Cut a small slash in the bottoms to hasten cooking. Steam 10 minutes or boil in water for 5 minutes. Do not overcook.

CABBAGE

Cut in wedges, and steam or boil in water for approximately 10 minutes.

CARROTS

Peel and cut up in slices, or sticks. Baby carrots may be kept whole. Steam or boil in water for about 10 minutes, or until tender.

CAULIFLOWER

Cut up and steam or boil for about 10 minutes. Do not overcook. Cauliflower may be cooked whole, if desired. Use a large pot and steam or boil for about 20 minutes. Cauliflower is best if served slightly crisp, not overcooked.

GREENS

Greens include bok choi, Swiss chard, collards, kale, beet tops, mustard greens, and turnip greens. Boil in a small amount of water for 5 to 10 minutes.

JICAMA

Peel, slice, and serve raw in salads, or with a dip.

KOHLRABI

Cut off leaves, pare, and cut up. Boil for about 20 minutes, or until tender.

LEEKS

Leeks are a member of the onion family. They are mostly used in soups. Leeks can be rather muddy. Slice leeks in half, in order to clean thoroughly. Boil or steam for about 8 minutes.

ONIONS

For boiling, use the small white ones, cover with water, and simmer for about 15 minutes, or until tender.

PARSNIPS

Peel and slice. Simmer about 10 minutes, or until tender.

PEAS

Boil or steam for 5 to 10 minutes.

POTATOES

The story that the best vitamins are nearest the skin of the potato is an old wives' tale. Potatoes should be peeled before cooking. Remove all green parts, as they are not good to eat. Boil potatoes, either whole or cut up, in water until tender—about 20 minutes in most cases.

RUTABAGAS

Peel, slice, and boil for about 20 minutes.

SPINACH

Wash well, spinach can be sandy. Steam or boil in a small amount of water for about 5 minutes. Do not overcook.

SQUASH, SPAGHETTI

Boil whole, in a large pot, for about 20 minutes, or longer, depending upon size of squash. The inside of this squash is filled with shreds that look like spaghetti.

SQUASH, SUMMER

Summer squashes include zucchini, yellow squash, and patty pans. Steam or boil in a small amount of water for 5 to 10 minutes. A teaspoon of oil may be added to boiling zucchini.

SQUASH, WINTER

Winter squashes include pumpkins, acorn squash, banana squash, butternut squash, and hubbard squash. Slice and boil for about 10 minutes. Squash may also be steamed for about 15 minutes. Acorn squash may be left whole, placed in the oven, and baked at 350° until tender, which will take about ½ to 1 hour, depending upon the size. Slice and remove seeds and peeling. Serve mashed, or in slices.

TURNIP

Cook like rutabagas.

YAMS AND SWEET POTATOES

Peel, slice, and boil for about 15 minutes, or until tender. May be baked, unpeeled, in a 350° or 400° oven for about 40 minutes to 1 hour, depending upon size.

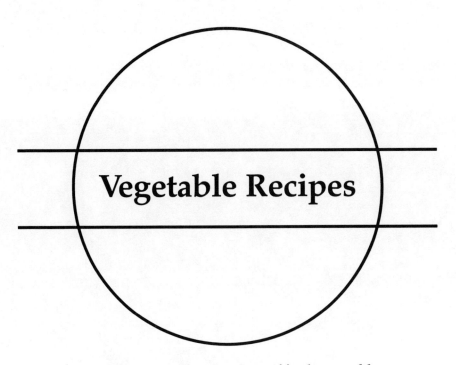

Vegetable Recipes

We can buy an amazing variety of fresh vegetables year-round. The secret of preparing delicious vegetables is to avoid overcooking.

BARLEY AND MUSHROOM CASSEROLE (PARVE)

This makes a nice change from potatoes or rice.

 2 T oil
 1 medium onion, chopped
 ½ c sliced mushrooms or 1 can (4 oz) mushrooms, drained
 ½ c pearl barley, washed
 2 c hot water
 2 tsp chicken-flavored soup powder
 ⅛ tsp pepper (or to taste)
 ½ tsp salt (optional)

Heat oil and cook onion until limp. Add mushrooms and barley, and stir over medium heat for 2 or 3 minutes. Stir in other ingredients. Cover, and bake at 350° for 1¼ to 1½ hours, until barley is tender. Stir a couple of times during cooking, and add a little more water if necessary. Serves four.

CABBAGE STIR FRY (PARVE)

This recipe is suitable for Passover.

    1 T oil
    1 small onion, chopped
    2 ribs celery, diced
    4 c shredded cabbage
    1 T parve chicken-flavored soup powder or 2 bouillon cubes
    ½ tsp salt
    dash of pepper
    dash of cumin (optional)
    ½ c hot water

Brown onion in the oil. Add all ingredients except water, and stir over high heat for 1 or 2 minutes. Add water, and cook, stirring, until vegetables are tender (this will only take a few moments). Serves six.

CARROTS, FRENCH STYLE (PARVE)

This recipe is suitable for Passover.

    2 c sliced carrots
    1 T sugar
    2 T margarine
    ½ c water
    dash of salt and pepper
    1 T chopped parsley

Place all ingredients except the parsley in a pan, cover and simmer until the water boils away. Let carrots cook until they are lightly browned. Sprinkle with the parsley. Serves four.

CARROT TZIMMES (PARVE)

This recipe is suitable for Passover and is traditional on Rosh
Hashanah.

1 T margarine
6 carrots, sliced
1 tsp lemon juice
1 tsp honey
salt to taste

Heat margarine over medium high heat and add carrots. Cook and
stir until carrots start to brown. Add lemon juice and honey, and
enough water to barely cover. Bring to boil, lower heat, cover pan,
and turn down heat. Simmer about 20 minutes, or until tender. Add
salt if desired. Serves five to six.

CORN AND TOMATOES

Whether this is parve or milk depends upon the bread crumbs.

nonstick spray
1 can (15 oz) corn, drained
1 can (14½ oz) stewed tomatoes
½ c fine bread crumbs
2 T margarine

Heat oven to 350°. Spray a 1½ quart-sized casserole with the nonstick spray. Drain the corn and spread in the bottom of the casserole. Spread the undrained stewed tomatoes on top. Sprinkle with
the crumbs and dot with the margarine. Bake for 30 minutes. Serves
four.

CORN ON THE COB

ears of corn—one or two for each person
water to cover
butter or margarine
salt and pepper

Bring water to boil in a large pot with a cover. Remove leaves and silk from the corn cobs. Wash off, and drop in the water. Cover and cook for 5 to 7 minutes. Remove from water and serve with butter, salt, and pepper.

FLORABEL'S VEGETABLE AND FRUIT KUGEL (PARVE)

This kugel contains no eggs. It is suitable for any holiday, including Passover.

½ c grated apple
½ c grated carrot
½ c grated potato
4 cut-up, pitted prunes
¼ c raisins
¼ c sugar
¼ c cracker crumbs or matzo meal
½ tsp cinnamon
¼ c vegetable oil
1 T lemon juice
¼ tsp salt

Mix all ingredients and place in an 8 by 8 inch pan. Bake at 350° for 50 minutes. Cut in squares and serve cold or hot. Serves six to eight.

FRIED GREEN TOMATOES

3–4 green or underripe tomatoes
1 egg, beaten (or egg substitute)
½ c fine bread or cracker crumbs
3 T oil

Slice the tomatoes about ½ inch thick. Heat oil in large pan. Dip the tomato slices in the egg. Place crumbs on a dish, and coat the tomato slices with them. Fry in the oil until brown on both sides. Serves three to four.

GREEN BEANS LYONNAISE (PARVE)

Rosemary or basil is good with green beans.

1 lb fresh or frozen green beans
1 onion, chopped
2 T margarine
salt and pepper

Steam green beans or cook in small amount of water, until tender. Meanwhile, saute the onion in the margarine until golden brown. Drain the beans and stir into the onions. Add salt and pepper and ½ teaspoon other herbs, if desired. Heat together about 5 minutes, stirring. Serves five.

HERBED POTATOES (PARVE)

2 T margarine or butter
1 medium onion, chopped
4 large potatoes
1½ c water
salt to taste
1 tsp dried parsley flakes or 1 T chopped fresh parsley
2 tsp marjoram
1 tsp oregano
1 tsp basil
(or substitute an Italian herb mix for the herbs)
1 clove garlic, minced (optional)

Heat margarine in a large pan. Add onion and garlic, and cook until they begin to brown. Meanwhile, peel and slice potatoes. Add and cook for 5 minutes, turning. Add all other ingredients. Cover, bring to a boil, and simmer for 30 minutes. Serves two to four.

IRA'S POTATOES (PARVE)

This recipe goes well with meat or fish. I usually make Baked Trout at the same time, cooking it for the last 20 minutes of the 40 minutes required for the potatoes. This recipe is suitable for Passover.

4 medium potatoes, peeled
1 medium onion
pepper and salt to taste
1 tsp dried parsley flakes or 1 T chopped fresh parsley
2 T oil
¾ c boiling water

Preheat oven to 425°. Slice potatoes and onion ¼ inch thick, and spread in a 9 by 13 inch pan. Top with remaining ingredients and bake for 40 minutes, or until potatoes brown on top. Serves two to four.

L.A. RICE (PARVE)

If rice-shaped pasta is not available in your market, break some spaghetti up into smallish bits.

¾ c rice
¼ c orzo (rice-shaped pasta)
2 tsp soup powder or 2 bouillon cubes (any flavor)
2 c water

Place all ingredients in a pot. Bring to boil. Turn down heat to low. Cover tightly and cook 20 minutes. Stir and serve.

Variations: Serve with a fried onion or fried mushrooms, or mix in ½ cup cooked vegetables, such as peas or diced carrots.

NOT-FRIED FRIES (PARVE)

Here is a recipe that not only saves on the calories over french fries, but is much more economical than buying frozen fries. This recipe is suitable for Passover.

4 potatoes
nonstick cooking spray

1 T water
1 T oil

Preheat oven to 450°. Peel and slice potatoes into strips. Place in a bowl and mix well with the water and oil. Spray a cookie sheet with the nonstick cooking spray, and spread the potatoes evenly over the surface. Bake 15 minutes, remove from oven and turn the potatoes. Cook 10 minutes longer, or until brown. Serves two or three (may be doubled if two cookie sheets will fit in the oven at one time).

Variation: For Chili Fries, top fries with ½ to 1 cup Frijoles, ¼ cup shredded cheese. Chopped onion (2 tablespoons) is optional.

ONION PICKLE (PARVE)

Save a bottle of pickle juice, after eating all the pickles.

1 large onion, sliced

Put the onion slices in the bottle, packing under the juice. Refrigerate for 3 days before eating.

ONION RELISH (PARVE)

Thinly sliced cucumber may be substituted for part of the onions in this recipe. These onions are just right for serving with hamburgers or fish.

2 c thinly sliced onion
½ c vinegar
1 T sugar
1 tsp celery seed
dash of pepper
½ tsp salt (optional)
¼ tsp prepared mustard
¼ c water

Place onions in a bowl. Combine other ingredients and pour over the onions. Refrigerate, covered, for at least 2 hours before serving. Stir before serving. Serves six.

OVEN EGGPLANT (PARVE)

This low-fat version of fried eggplant not only uses much less oil, it is much easier to make. For economy, it can be baked in the oven the same time as other foods, such as chicken. This recipe is suitable for Passover.

    1 large or 2 small eggplants
    nonstick spray
    2 T oil
    1 egg, beaten (or use egg substitute)
    ½ c fine bread crumbs or matzo meal
    dash of salt (optional)

Slice the eggplant (unpeeled) into ½ inch slices. Spray a large, flat pan or cookie sheet that has sides with the nonstick spray and then put in the oil. Dip the eggplant slices in the egg and then coat with the crumbs, which have been placed on a plate. Position the eggplant in a single layer in the pan. Bake at 350° oven for 15 minutes. Remove from oven and turn the eggplant slices over, then return it to the oven for 15 minutes more. Serves three.

OVEN-HASHED POTATOES (PARVE)

This is easier than frying, and it uses a lot less fat. This recipe is suitable for Passover.

    4 c (about 4 small) grated potatoes
    ½ onion, grated
    2 T oil
    salt and pepper to taste
    ½ c boiling water
    nonstick cooking spray

Spray a 9 by 13 inch pan with the nonstick cooking spray. Mix ingredients and spread in the pan. Place in a 425° oven and bake about 40 minutes, or until browned. Serves four.

PANNED GREEN BEANS (PARVE)

Figure one handful of green beans per person—the quarter pound
is an approximate amount.

1 T oil
approximately ¼ lb green beans, with ends trimmed off
1 medium onion, sliced
1 clove garlic, minced (optional)

Heat oil in pan. Add vegetables. Cook, stirring occasionally, over
medium heat, for 5 to 10 minutes. Serves three to four.

PARSNIPS, CARROTS, AND CELERY (PARVE)

This recipe is suitable for Passover.

1 T margarine
4 parsnips
2 carrots
2 ribs celery (with leaves)
1 small onion
1 tsp rosemary or a sprig of fresh rosemary
dash of pepper
¼ to ½ tsp salt (optional)
½ c water

Slice vegetables. Heat margarine and lightly brown vegetables. Add
other ingredients and cover. Simmer until tender, about 15 minutes,
then uncover and cook 5 minutes more. Serves four.

Variations: Use all carrots instead of the parsnips. Instead of rosemary, you can use parsley flakes or a sprig of fresh parsley.

PICKLED VEGETABLES (PARVE)

Excellent to serve with meat, turkey, chicken, or sandwiches. Good make-ahead dish if you are expecting company, or before big holidays.

An assortment of sliced vegetables:
carrots, zucchini, cauliflower, onions, cucumbers, green toma-
toes, green beans, bell peppers (enough to fill a quart jar)

Brine:
1¼ c water (bottled, distilled water is best)
1 c white vinegar
1½ T noniodized or kosher salt
2 tsp pickling spice
2 dried hot peppers
2 cloves garlic
2 sprigs fresh parsley

Pack the vegetables in a wide-mouth, heat-resistant, glass quart jar. Heat the brine ingredients to boiling. Boil for 1 minute. Pour the brine into the vegetables. Allow to cool, cover tightly, and refrigerate. These are ready to eat in five days and will keep for two months in the refrigerator.

POTATO CASSEROLE (PARVE)

The potato casserole can be put into the oven at the same time as some other dish, such as chicken or meat. This recipe is suitable for Passover.

5 medium potatoes
3 small or 2 large carrots
nonstick spray
2 T margarine
1 medium to large onion, diced
½ bell pepper, diced
1–2 cloves garlic, minced
1 rib celery, sliced

dash of salt
½ tsp paprika

Peel and slice the potatoes and carrots, put in a pot with water to cover, and bring to boil. Simmer 20 minutes, or until tender. Spray a large frying pan, and add the margarine and other vegetables. Cook over medium heat until onion browns on the edges. Drain and mash the potatoes and carrots. Spray a casserole and line the bottom with half the potato mixture. Cover with the onion mixture, and sprinkle on the salt, if desired. Top with the remaining potato mixture, and smooth with the back of a spoon. Sprinkle the paprika on top, and bake in a 350° oven, covered, for 45 minutes to 1 hour. Serves four to six.

Variation: Instead of potatoes, may be made with 2 pounds of yams or sweet potatoes—omit the celery.

POTATOES BLOSSOM (PARVE)

This is a bit of a bother. I usually hate recipes that call for use of more than one pan—but this is worth it. If you want, you could use a pan that will go from the top of the stove into the oven for this dish, though, and there you are! Just cook and drain the potatoes, then mix in the other ingredients.

4–5 large potatoes, peeled and diced
½ onion, sliced
1 rib celery, diced
¼ c margarine or butter
1 tsp dried parsley flakes or 1 T chopped fresh parsley
1 tsp salt
pepper to taste
1 tsp poultry seasoning

Place potatoes in a saucepan, cover with water, and bring to a boil. Meanwhile, spread the margarine over the bottom of a 9 by 13 pan. Add all other ingredients. Let potatoes boil for 5 to 10 minutes. Drain. Add potatoes to other ingredients in pan. Bake in 375° oven for 30 minutes, or until vegetables are tender. Serves four.

POTATOES HERMAN (MILK)

If cholesterol is no problem at your house, you can add margarine or butter to the mashed potatoes. If cholesterol is a consideration, add no margarine and use low-fat cheese. This recipe is suitable for Passover.

    4–5 potatoes, cooked and mashed
    1 large onion, sliced
    ½ bell pepper, diced
    1 T oil
    salt and pepper
    3 slices American or cheddar cheese, or use grated cheese
    nonstick spray

Heat oil in large pan and saute the onion and bell pepper until browned. Stir the onion mixture with the potatoes, and mix in one slice of cheese, which has been cut up. Add salt and pepper to taste. Place in a casserole, that has been sprayed with nonstick spray, and top with remaining cheese. Bake at 400° for 20 to 30 minutes, until cheese is melted and edges start to brown. Serves four.

POTATO LATKES (PARVE)

Good with applesauce or sour cream. Traditionally served on Chanukah.

    5 potatoes
    2 eggs, beaten
    1 T matzo meal
    ½ tsp salt
    1 tsp baking powder
    pepper
    small amount of grated onion (to taste)
    oil or nonstick spray

Peel potatoes, and grate. Drain off liquid. Mix in eggs, and other ingredients except oil. Drop by tablespoons on a hot pan that has been greased with oil or nonstick spray, and fry. Serves six.

POTATO PATTIES (PARVE)

This is a nonfat recipe; but instead of baking, the potato patties can be fried in oil or fat until browned on both sides. This recipe may be used on Passover.

  4 medium potatoes, cooked and mashed
  dash of salt and pepper
  ½ tsp onion powder (or 1 T fresh grated onion)
  2 egg whites
  ½ c matzo meal (approximately)
  nonstick spray

Set oven at 400°. Mix potatoes with salt, pepper, onion powder, and egg whites. Form into patties. Put matzo meal on a plate, and coat the patties in it. Place them in a flat pan. Bake for 15 minutes, turn, and bake 15 minutes more. Serves three to four.

RED BEANS (PARVE)

Red beans and rice is a popular food in Louisiana, and is cooked here as a vegetarian dish.

  1 lb dried red beans
  4 c water
  1 T oil
  1 onion, diced
  2 cloves garlic, minced
  salt to taste
  ¼–½ tsp hot sauce (or as much as you like)
  2 c cooked rice (optional)

Wash beans, and cover with the water. Bring to boil. Boil 5 minutes. Turn off heat, and leave to stand, covered, for 1 hour. Cook the onion and garlic in the oil, until browned on the edges. Add to beans. Heat to boiling. Turn down heat, and simmer for about 2 hours, or until tender, adding more water if necessary. Stir in salt and hot sauce. Serves six to eight.

RED CABBAGE, SWEET AND SOUR (PARVE)

Serve this as a hot or cold vegetable, or as a salad or relish. It is a good accompaniment for roast beef, turkey, or fish.

1 small red cabbage, shredded
1 c applesauce
3 T vinegar
½ c water
3 T brown sugar
1 tsp salt
dash of pepper

Place all ingredients in a pot, stir, cover, and bring to a boil. Lower heat and simmer for 20 minutes, stirring occasionally. Serve hot or cold. Serves six.

RICE AND PEAS (PARVE)

1 c rice, cooked
½ c peas, cooked
pepper, to taste
½ tsp salt

Combine some cooked rice and cooked peas, or some canned peas. Warm and serve. Serves three or four.

RICE PILAF (PARVE)

If you would like to make rice pilaf with brown rice, adjust cooking time and amount of water, according to package directions. An equal amount of chicken or beef soup may be used instead of the water and soup powder.

1 T oil or margarine
1 c uncooked white rice
1 small onion, finely chopped

2 c water
2 tsp chicken or beef-flavored soup powder
salt and pepper to taste

Heat oil and lightly brown onion. Add rice and stir for 2 or 3 minutes over medium heat. Add other ingredients, and bring to boil. Lower heat, cover, and simmer on low heat for 20 minutes. Stir before serving. Serves four.

ROAST VEGETABLES (PARVE)

No problems here—just add or subtract different vegetables as you wish. Rutabagas, parsnips, or any root vegetables may be used. These vegetables will cook in the oven along with a chicken or other oven dish. This recipe is suitable for Passover.

2–3 potatoes
2–3 carrots
2–3 parsnips
1 small turnip
1 onion
3 cloves of garlic, peeled
2 T oil
salt and pepper to taste
1 tsp parsley flakes, or sprig of fresh parsley
1 tsp rosemary, or sprig of fresh rosemary
nonstick spray
¼ c hot water

Peel and slice vegetables. Add oil, water, herbs, salt and pepper. Bake, covered, at 350° in a pan that has been sprayed with nonstick spray, until done (about 45 minutes). Serves six.

RUTABAGA AND POTATOES (PARVE)

Here's where your trusty potato masher comes in handy. Rutabagas are an underappreciated vegetable. They are very tasty and
supply vitamins A and C. My husband once grew a row of rutabagas in the back of the flower bed. Many people stopped by our house
to ask what those lovely foliage plants were. This recipe is suitable
for Passover.

1 large rutabaga, peeled and diced
4 potatoes, peeled and sliced
salt and pepper to taste
2 T butter or margarine

Cook the rutabaga and potatoes in boiling water until tender, about
20 minutes. Drain. Add salt, pepper and margarine, and mash well.
Serves six.

STEWED TOMATOES

This is an old-fashioned American dish.

4 c canned tomatoes, drained and diced
½ green pepper, diced (or use frozen diced peppers)
½ small onion, chopped fine
1½ c soft bread crumbs
dash of pepper
½ tsp salt (optional)
1 tsp sugar
½ tsp basil
¼ c margarine or butter

Preheat oven to 400°. Place half the bread crumbs in bottom of 1½
quart glass baking dish. Cover with the other ingredients except for
the margarine or butter, and crumbs. Top with the remaining bread
crumbs. Cut margarine into cubes and scatter on top, then bake for
25 minutes. Serves four.

SUCCOTASH

Corn and beans is an American classic food, and pioneer women even named a patchwork quilt pattern, "Corn and Beans." The name *succotash* comes from the Narraganset Indians.

1 c frozen lima beans
1 c frozen corn
1 T butter or margarine
salt and pepper

Cover frozen lima beans and corn with water. Bring to a boil and boil for 8 to 10 minutes. Drain, then add butter, salt, and pepper. Serves four. May be made in any quantity.

TOMATO RELISH (PARVE)

It is very good with fish, hamburger, mashed potatoes, or chicken.

2 T oil
1 large onion, diced
1 green pepper, diced, or use frozen diced peppers
1 large can (28 oz) peeled tomatoes
dash pepper
1 tsp sugar
2 T vinegar
1 tsp prepared mustard

Heat oil in a large skillet, add onion, and cook, stirring, until the edges start to brown, about 5 minutes. Add peppers and cook 3 minutes more. Drain the tomatoes, and cut up (save the juice for soup or some other recipe). Add all ingredients to the onions and mix well. Simmer 5 minutes more, or until very thick. Serve hot or cold.

VEGETABLE TZIMMES (PARVE)

Without too much fuss! This recipe is suitable for Passover.

**4 carrots, sliced
3 sweet potatoes, sliced
3 small cooking apples, peeled and thinly sliced
½ c honey
salt and pepper to taste
3 T margarine
½ c pitted prunes
1 c water**

Cook the carrots and sweet potatoes until tender, and then drain. Mix all ingredients in a large baking dish. Cover and bake at 350° for 30 minutes. Serves six to eight.

YAM OR SWEET POTATO MASH (PARVE)

This recipe goes well with turkey. It is suitable for Passover, or other holidays.

**3–4 medium yams
3 T brown sugar or white sugar
2 T margarine
grated rind of one orange
¼ c orange juice
dash of salt and pepper**

Peel yams, and slice them. Place in a pot and cover with water. Cover the pot, and bring to a boil. Lower heat, and simmer ½ hour, or until tender. Drain and add other ingredients. Mash the yams. Serves six.

ZUCCHINI IN TOMATO SAUCE (PARVE)

1 can (14½ oz) stewed tomatoes
2 small zucchini, sliced
½ tsp basil
¼ tsp garlic powder
½ tsp oregano or Italian seasoning (optional)
salt and pepper to taste

Heat all ingredients to boiling. Lower heat and simmer for 15 minutes, or until zucchini is tender. Serve hot or cold. Serves three to four.

ZUCCHINI KUGEL (PARVE)

This is an excellent accompaniment to meat or chicken, and a good way to use up one of those zucchini that "got away" hiding under the leaves in the garden, and growing bigger than desired! Vegetables may be grated in the food processor.

1 large zucchini, or 3 regular-size zucchini, grated
1 small onion, grated
1 egg plus one egg white, beaten (or use egg substitute)
3 T flour
dash of pepper
½ tsp baking powder
½ tsp salt

Mix all ingredients and put in a greased 8 by 8 inch pan. Bake at 350° for 40 minutes, until edges brown. Serves six.

ZUCCHINI STEW (MILK)

2 T oil
1 rib celery, sliced
1 carrot, sliced
½ green pepper, diced
2–3 small potatoes, peeled and diced
3 small zucchini, diced
1 small onion, diced
1 tomato, diced
1 clove of garlic, minced
1 tsp oregano
½ tsp basil
salt and pepper to taste
1 can (8 oz) tomato sauce
grated Parmesan cheese

Heat oil and add vegetables. Cook, stirring, over medium high heat for 5 to 10 minutes. Add oregano, basil, seasonings, and tomato sauce. Lower heat, cover, and simmer for about 25 minutes. Sprinkle with cheese before serving. Serves four.

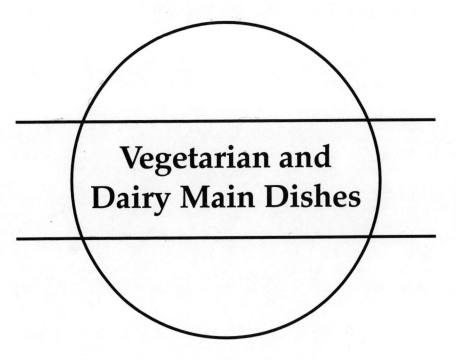

Vegetarian and Dairy Main Dishes

Better a meal of vegetables where there is love
Than a fattened ox where there is hate.

Proverbs 15:17
(THE WRITINGS—KETHUBIM
[Jewish Publication Society])

AUNT EVELYN'S NOODLE PUDDING (MILK)

A delectable kugel for those special events in life, and one of the few recipes in this book calling for a lot of cream!

1 lb broad noodles
3 eggs, beaten
1 pint sour cream
1 lb pot cheese or cottage cheese
¼ c sugar
2 c milk
1 tsp cinnamon, mixed with 1 T sugar

Break up noodles and boil for 8 minutes. Drain and rinse, and return them to the pot. Stir in eggs, add sour cream, pot or cottage cheese, ¼ c sugar, and milk. Mix well. Grease a 9 by 13 pan with butter or margarine. Pour mixture into pan and sprinkle cinnamon and sugar mixture over top. Bake at 425° for 1 hour. Cool on rack for 15 minutes to set, then cut in squares. Serve warm or cold. Serves eight.

BAKED BEANS (PARVE)

Without all the syrupy sweetness and fat of ordinary bean recipes, this is a flavorful vegetable.

    2 c dried pinto beans or red beans
    1 T vinegar
    1 can (8 oz) tomato sauce
    ¼ of an onion, chopped
    1 T oil
    2 tsp salt (optional)
    1 tsp powdered mustard
    dash of pepper

Place beans in a large pot and cover with water. Boil for 3 to 5 minutes. Turn off heat, cover pot, and let sit for 1 hour. Add more hot water if necessary, and simmer for 1 hour. Then add all ingredients and mix well. Place in a casserole and bake in the oven at 300° for 2 to 3 hours, or until beans are tender—do not cover while baking. Stir and add hot water during baking, if needed. Serves six to eight.

BAKED ZITI (MILK)

Ziti is a lovely, fat type of macaroni—plus a useful word for word games.

    8 oz ziti or large macaroni
    1 T oil
    1 onion, diced
    1 clove garlic, minced
    4–5 mushrooms, sliced (optional)
    1 can (6 oz) tomato paste
    1 tsp oregano
    ½ tsp basil
    ½ tsp salt
    1 c water
    8 oz ricotta cheese
    3 slices of mozzarella cheese
    ¼ c grated Parmesan cheese

Cook ziti according to package instructions, and drain. For the sauce, cook the onion, mushrooms, and garlic in the oil until browned. Add the other ingredients except the cheeses and simmer for 15 minutes over low heat. Place ziti in a casserole and top with the ricotta and mozzarella cheeses. Pour sauce mixture over top, and sprinkle with the Parmesan cheese. Bake at 350° for 20 minutes.

Variation: Bottled spaghetti sauce (1½ to 2 cups) may be substituted for the tomato paste and onion mixture.

BEAN AND RICE PILAF (PARVE)

1 T oil
1 onion, chopped
1 clove garlic, minced
1 c raw white rice
2 c hot water
1 can (15 oz) kidney beans, drained, or 2 c cooked beans
2 tsp soup powder or 2 bouillon cubes
pepper
½ tsp celery salt

Heat oil, add garlic and onion, and cook until browned. Stir in rice. Add other ingredients, cover, and bring to a boil. Lower heat and simmer, covered, for 20 minutes. Serves three to four.

BEAN BARBECUE (MILK)

This recipe is easier to make if you have a food processor or blender.
Bottled barbecue sauce may be substituted for the sauce recipe listed
here. Serve with potatoes or rice.

1 T onion, chopped
2 T green pepper, chopped
1 T oil
1 can (16 oz) vegetarian beans in tomato sauce
dash of pepper
¼ tsp prepared mustard
½ tsp Worcestershire sauce
1 egg, beaten, or egg substitute
1 c dry bread crumbs or matzo meal
¼ c milk
nonstick spray

Grease or spray with nonstick spray, a 1½ quart glass baking pan
or similar casserole dish. Heat the oil in a skillet and cook the onion
and green pepper until tender. Mash the beans or grind in a food
processor. Mix all ingredients and spread in the pan. Bake at 350°
for 20 minutes.

The Sauce:
1 T oil
½ small onion, chopped
1 clove garlic, minced
1 rib celery, diced
½ c ketchup
1 T vinegar
1 tsp Worcestershire sauce
1 T molasses
1 tsp prepared mustard
dash of pepper
½ c water

Heat oil, add onion, garlic, and celery, and cook until browned. Add
all other ingredients, stir, and heat to boiling. Lower heat and simmer for 15 minutes. Serve with the beans.

BEAN BURGERS (PARVE)

Serve with ketchup or tomato sauce.

> 2 c cooked pinto beans, drained (or substitute plain
>   canned beans)
> salt and pepper to taste
> 1 egg, beaten
> 1 T fine bread crumbs
> ½ tsp parsley flakes
> 2 T oil

Mash beans. Mix all ingredients except oil. Heat oil in pan. Form mixture into patties, and brown on each side. Makes 5 or 6 burgers.

BROWN RICE AND BEANS CASSEROLE (MILK)

> 1 T oil
> ½ large onion, red or yellow, diced
> ½ bell pepper, diced
> 2 garlic cloves, minced
> 1 tsp oregano
> ¼–½ tsp chili powder (optional)
> 1 c cooked brown rice (½ c raw)
> 1 can (15 oz) plain pinto beans, drained, or 2 c cooked beans
> 1 slice cheese

Cook the brown rice—regular or quick-cooking type—according to the package directions. While the rice is cooking, brown the onions, bell pepper, and garlic in the oil. Turn off the heat, and add the oregano, chili powder, and the beans. Mix the rice and bean mixture in a casserole. Top with a cheese slice. Bake 20 minutes at 350°. Serves three.

BUTTER BEAN LOAF (MILK)

Butter bean is another name for *lima bean*.

1 can (15 oz) butter beans or limas, or 2 c cooked beans
1 ½ c bread crumbs
1 c milk
1 egg, slightly beaten
1 T margarine or oil
pepper
½ tsp dried parsley
1 rib celery, chopped
1 small onion, diced (optional)
nonstick spray

Grease a 7 by 12 inch glass baking pan, or spray with nonstick cooking spray. Mash beans. Mix ingredients and spread in pan. Bake in 350° oven for about 30 minutes. Serves three.

BUTTER BEANS AND RICE CASSEROLE (PARVE)

1 can (15 oz) vegetarian cooked dried butter (lima) beans (or
**   kidney beans), drained, or 2 c home cooked beans**
½ c raw white rice
½ onion, sliced
1 clove garlic, minced
2 small zucchini or other summer squash, sliced
1–2 carrots, sliced
1 rib celery, sliced
salt and pepper
1 tsp dried parsley flakes or 1 T chopped fresh parsley
½ tsp thyme
2 c boiling water

Preheat oven to 350°. Boil the water while assembling casserole. Mix all ingredients, cover and bake for 45 minutes. Stir and serve. Serves four.

Variation: Instead of baking, this dish may be prepared on top of the stove. Simmer over low heat for 20 minutes, or until rice is tender.

CORN AND BEANS CASSEROLE (MILK)

You can chop green peppers, celery, and onion in the food processor, using 1 thick slice each of the green pepper and onion.

> 1 can (15 oz) kidney beans, drained, or 2 c home-cooked beans
> 1 can (16 oz) cream-style corn
> ¼ c diced green pepper (fresh or frozen)
> 1 rib celery, sliced
> ¼ c chopped onion
> ¼ c mayonnaise
> 2 slices American or cheddar cheese
> 1 slice bread
> 1 T margarine

Preheat oven to 350°. Combine vegetables and mayonnaise. Place in a 10 by 6 glass baking dish. Top with cheese slices. Generously butter the bread with the margarine, and cut it up into little cubes. Toss on top of the casserole. Bake for 30 minutes. Serves four to six as a side dish, or two to three as a main dish.

CORN AND ZUCCHINI STEW (MILK)

> 1 can (16 oz) corn, drained
> 3 zucchini, diced
> 1 c nonfat (skim) milk
> ¼ onion, grated or chopped fine
> dash of pepper
> salt, if desired
> 1 c diced mozzarella cheese
> grated Parmesan cheese to taste

Place all ingredients except cheese in a saucepan and bring to a boil. Cover and lower heat. Simmer for 5 to 10 minutes, until zucchini is tender. Stir in cheese until it melts. Serves three to four.

CURRY (PARVE)

Curry is usually served with rice.

    1 T oil
    1 onion, chopped
    1 apple, diced
    1 can (16 oz) tomatoes
    1 can (15 oz) butter beans, drained, or 2 c cooked beans
    1 tsp curry powder
    1 bouillon cube or 1 tsp soup powder

Heat oil, and cook onion in it until brown. Add the apple. Cut up
tomatoes and stir in, adding the liquid from the can. Add all other
ingredients. Simmer for 20 minutes. Serves four.

EGGPLANT PARMESAN (MILK)

There are two ways to make this recipe. A can or bottle of spaghetti
sauce may be substituted for the tomato sauce and oregano, and the
garlic and onion mixture may be omitted, if desired.

    1 medium eggplant
    ¼ c mayonnaise (low-calorie can be used)
    1 c fine bread crumbs or matzo meal
    1 T oil
    1 onion, chopped
    1 clove of garlic, minced
    ½ bell pepper, diced (or use the frozen, diced bell pepper)
    4–5 mushrooms, sliced (optional)
    1 c (15 oz) tomato sauce
    1 tsp oregano
    salt and pepper to taste
    8 oz mozzarella cheese, sliced (nonfat can be used)
    ¼ c grated Parmesan cheese

Preheat oven to 425°. Cut eggplant into ½ inch slices. Mix bread
crumbs with part of the Parmesan cheese. Using a knife, spread the
mayonnaise on the eggplant, and dip each slice in the crumbs. Place

on an ungreased cookie sheet. Bake for 15 minutes. Heat the oil in a pan, and brown the onion, garlic, bell pepper, and mushrooms. Remove the eggplant from oven, and lower the heat to 375°. Place the eggplant in a 9 by 13 inch pan. Top with the mozzarella cheese and onion mixture. Add oregano, salt, and pepper. Top with the tomato sauce, remaining Parmesan cheese, and leftover crumbs. Bake for 15 minutes more. Serves three to four.

FRIJOLES (PARVE)

This is the California version of refried beans. The burritos mentioned in the recipe would make a dairy dish.

> 2 c cooked pinto beans (or 1 can [15 oz] pintos, drained)
> 2 T oil
> 1 large onion, diced
> 1 clove garlic, minced
> 1 can (8 oz) tomato sauce
> ½ tsp oregano
> ½ tsp chili powder (or to taste)
> 1 tsp salt (optional)

Heat oil, add onion and garlic, and cook until onion begins to brown. Lower heat and gradually add beans, mashing them with a fork or spatula. Add other ingredients and stir and simmer 5 more minutes.

Variation: Serve with rice, shredded lettuce, grated cheese, salsa, and tortillas. To make a burrito, spread a tortilla with the beans and add 1 to 2 tablespoons grated cheese. Fold the tortilla into a little package, and serve with salsa or hot taco sauce.

KIDNEY BEAN STEW (MILK)

2 T oil
1 onion
1 clove garlic, minced
1 medium zucchini or summer squash
1 large tomato
½ tsp thyme
1 can (15 oz) kidney beans, drained, or 2 c cooked beans
8 oz macaroni, cooked and drained
grated Parmesan cheese
salt and pepper

Heat oil. Dice onion, zucchini, and tomato, and cook along with the garlic and thyme, stirring, for about 15 minutes. Add macaroni and kidney beans. Stir over heat a few minutes, until beans are warmed. Sprinkle with the cheese and seasonings. Serves four.

LENTILS (PARVE)

Lentils do not require presoaking.

1 c lentils
3 c water
1 large onion, chopped
1 T oil
1 clove garlic, minced
1 tsp poultry seasoning
salt and pepper to taste.

Brown onion and garlic in oil, in a large pot. Wash lentils in a sieve and add to onions. Add poultry seasoning and water and bring to a boil. Lower heat and simmer about 50 minutes. Add more water during cooking, if necessary. Add salt and pepper if desired. Serves four to six.

LENTILS AND RICE (PARVE)

Lentils are quick to cook and do not require presoaking. This is a recipe for an Israeli dish called *Mejedrah*, which is often served on holidays.

2 T margarine or oil
2 green onions, sliced
2 carrots, sliced
1 rib celery, sliced
3–4 mushrooms, sliced (optional)
¼ green pepper, sliced
3 c water
2 tsp soup powder or 2 bouillon cubes
dash pepper
1 c lentils
½ c white rice (uncooked)
1 tsp salt (optional)

In medium saucepan, saute the green onion, carrots, celery, mushrooms, and green pepper in the margarine. Add water, soup powder, pepper, and lentils. Bring to boil. Cover and simmer 25 minutes. Stir in rice. Cover and simmer 20 more minutes, or until rice and lentils are tender. Add salt if desired. Serves four.

LENTILS WITH BARLEY (PARVE)

2 T oil
1 small chopped onion
1 rib celery, chopped
1 can (16 oz) tomatoes, sliced
2 c water
½ c lentils
1/3 c pearl barley
½ tsp salt
dash of pepper
¼ tsp rosemary
1 carrot, grated

In large pan, heat the oil and saute the onion and celery for 5 to 10 minutes over medium heat. Add all ingredients and bring to a boil. Turn heat to simmer, cover, and cook about ½ hour, or until barley and lentils are tender. Serves three.

MACARONI AND CHEESE (MILK)

6 c boiling water
2 c macaroni
5 slices American cheese, cut up
pepper
1 T margarine or butter
¾ c milk
1 T dry potato flakes (the kind for making instant potatoes)

Cook macaroni in the boiling water for 10 minutes. Drain and put margarine in a casserole. Add other ingredients and mix. Bake in a 350° oven for 30 minutes. Serves four.

MAC CHILI

This casserole may be prepared in advance and heated just before serving. Leftover cooked macaroni may be used. This may be a dairy dish, if the cheese is added, or parve, without it.

8 oz large macaroni shells
1 T oil
2 tsp dried onion flakes
½ tsp garlic powder
1 tsp chili powder (or to taste)
¼ tsp cumin
½ tsp basil
1 tsp oregano
⅓ cup frozen bell pepper, or some chopped fresh pepper
1 can (15 oz) pinto beans, drained, or 2 c cooked beans
1 can (15 oz) tomato sauce
2–3 slices American cheese, cut up, or grated cheese (optional)

Cook macaroni according to package directions and drain. Heat oven to 350°. Spread oil on bottom of a 9 by 13 inch pan. Mix in all ingredients except cheese. Bake for 30 minutes, or until heated through. Top with the cheese, if used, and serve hot. Serves four.

MEATLESS *CHOLENT* (PARVE)

This is the Jewish version of baked beans. It is a dish that can be kept warm for hours, while the family is at Sabbath services, and be ready to eat on returning home. The beans combined with the barley (a grain) form a complete protein.

1 c dried lima or great northern beans
2 T oil
1 large onion, sliced
1 clove of garlic, minced
½ tsp salt
dash of pepper
¼ c barley
2 large carrots, cut in chunks
2 large or 3 small potatoes, peeled and cut up
1 tsp paprika
2 tsp soup powder or 2 bouillon cubes (chicken or beef flavor)
hot water
Dumplings or Matzo Balls (optional)

Wash beans and cover generously with water. Bring to a boil and boil for 5 minutes. Turn off the heat, and let beans stand, covered, for 1 hour. Brown the onion and garlic in the oil. Add to beans, along with other ingredients. Pour over enough hot water to cover and bring to a boil. Turn heat to low, and simmer for 1½ hours, or until beans are tender; add more water during cooking if necessary (*cholent* should be thick). Serves four. Dumplings may be added if desired.

Dumplings (Milk)

This recipe calls for milk. For a parve dumpling, see the recipe for *Cholent* in the Meat chapter, or make Matzo Balls.

1 c flour
2 tsp baking powder
½ tsp salt
dash of pepper
½ c milk

Mix dry ingredients and then stir in milk. Lightly form into balls or drop from tablespoon onto simmering food. Cover tightly and cook for 20 minutes. Do not peek during cooking.

MEATLESS LASAGNA (MILK)

8 oz pkg lasagna noodles
2 T oil
1 large onion, diced
1 clove garlic, minced
¼ c bell pepper, diced
1 tsp oregano
½ tsp thyme or basil
1 can (15 oz) tomato sauce
1 can (14½ oz) stewed tomatoes
15 oz ricotta cheese
6–8 oz sliced mozzarella cheese
grated Parmesan cheese
nonstick spray

Boil the lasagna noodles in a large pot of water, according to package directions. Drain. Heat the oil, and brown the onion and garlic. Add the bell pepper, oregano, thyme, tomato sauce, and stewed tomatoes. Heat to boiling, lower heat, and simmer for 10 to 15 minutes. Grease a 9 by 13 inch pan, or spray it with nonstick spray. Cover the bottom with 3 lasagna noodles. Top the noodles with half of the ricotta cheese, part of the sauce, and some of the mozzarella slices. Repeat the layering process once more—there should be 3 layers of the noodles. Top with the remaining tomato sauce and mozzarella cheese, and sprinkle with Parmesan cheese. At this point, the casserole may be refrigerated for heating later or baked at 350° for about 30 minutes. Serves eight.

Variations: For Spinach Lasagna, add 1 cup chopped cooked spinach (fresh or frozen) to the cheese, along with 2 tablespoons chopped fresh parsley and ¼ cup sliced, roasted almonds. For Vegetable Lasagna, add 1 rib celery (sliced) and 1 cup frozen mixed vegetables to the sauce mixture.

MEATLESS SPAGHETTI SAUCE

It's true that store shelves are lined with many different brands of spaghetti sauce, but your own has less sodium and no preservatives, and it costs much less. It will cook while you are making the spaghetti, so the store-bought sauce hardly saves you much time, either. If unexpected guests arrive, stretch out the sauce with a 6 ounce can of tomato paste combined with water or a 16 ounce can of tomatoes. This recipe calls for cheese, but the cheese may be omitted for a parve meal or when serving meat or chicken at the same time.

1 T oil
1 clove garlic, minced
1 onion, diced
1 can (15 oz) tomato sauce
1 tsp oregano
dash of pepper
1 tsp salt (optional)
½ tsp thyme
1 small tomato, diced
½ green pepper, diced (optional)
3–4 mushrooms, diced (optional)
grated Parmesan cheese (optional)
8 oz spaghetti, cooked

Heat oil and cook onion and garlic until onion is tender. Add other ingredients except cheese and spaghetti, and heat to boiling. Lower heat and simmer for 20 minutes. Cook spaghetti according to package directions and drain. Serve spaghetti with the sauce and sprinkle top with the Parmesan cheese (if used). Serves four.

PIZZA PIE (MILK)

Very easy, and you can have your choice of toppings! My niece Leslie likes it best with mushrooms on top.

Dough:
1 pkg dried yeast
¾ c warm water
1 T oil
1 tsp sugar
1 tsp salt
2 c all-purpose flour

Sauce:
1 can (8 oz) tomato sauce
¼–½ c sliced or grated mozzarella cheese
1–2 T grated Parmesan cheese
½ tsp oregano (or to taste)
dash of pepper
½ tsp basil or parsley
your choice of ¼ c sliced mushrooms, chopped tomato, bell
    pepper, onions, and so forth
nonstick spray

Mix together the dough ingredients. Be very careful about the temperature of the water—it should be warm, but not too hot, or you will kill your yeast. Test it on your arm, like a baby bottle. Knead the dough until smooth, cover, and place in a warm place to rise for about an hour.

Heat the oven to 450°. Grease a 12½ to 13 inch round pizza pan, or cookie sheet, or a square pan, or it may be sprayed with nonstick spray. Spread out the dough right up over the edges. Cover the dough with the sauce, cheese, and other ingredients. Bake for 20 minutes. Serves four.

POTATO PIE (MILK)

1 T oil
1 onion, chopped
3 potatoes, peeled and grated
1 tsp dried parsley or 1 T chopped fresh parsley
½ tsp paprika
¼ tsp salt, or to taste
dash of pepper
2 eggs, beaten (or egg substitute)
1 c milk (regular or skim)
2 slices Swiss cheese, cut up

Fry the onion in the oil until browned. Place grated potatoes in the bottom of a large pie pan and top with the onions. Sprinkle with the seasonings and place cheese on top. Mix egg and milk and pour over. Bake at 375° for 40 minutes, or until done. Let set about 10 minutes before serving. Serves four.

SOY BEAN CASSEROLE (MILK)

Soy beans are one of the most nourishing of beans, having more protein than the others. When cooked, they are a bit more crunchy than other beans.

1 c dried soybeans
4 c water
1 can (16 oz) cream-style corn
1 can (16 oz) tomatoes (sliced up)
1 tsp sugar
salt and pepper to taste
¼ tsp marjoram
2 tsp margarine
1 slice bread
2 slices American cheese

Wash beans. Place in a pot and add the water. Cover and bring to boil. Boil 5 minutes, then turn off the heat and let stand, covered, for 1 hour. Bring to a boil again, turn down heat, and simmer until tender (about 2 to 3 hours). Drain beans and mix with sugar, corn, and tomatoes. Place in a shallow casserole and top with cheese. Spread margarine on the slice of bread and cut the bread into cubes, then put it on top of the casserole. Add seasonings and bake at 375° for 30 minutes. Serves six.

SOY RICE DINNER (PARVE)

The soy bean is frequently used in Oriental cooking. Soy granules are ground up soy beans.

  2 T oil
  1 medium onion, chopped
  2 carrots, sliced
  1 rib celery, sliced
  1 clove garlic, minced
  1 tsp dried parsley flakes
  1 tsp thyme
  1 c uncooked rice (white or quick-cooking brown)
  dash of pepper
  1 c soy granules
  2 T soy sauce
  1 T Worcestershire sauce (optional)
  3½ c water

Heat oil in large pot. Add vegetables and garlic and cook over medium heat until the onion starts to brown. Add all other ingredients and bring to a boil. Lower heat and cover. Simmer 25 minutes, adding more hot water if necessary. Serves four to six.

SPAGHETTI PIZZA PIE (MILK)

No bread crust for this pizza—instead there is a layer of spaghetti on the bottom.

  8 oz spaghetti, cooked
  2 eggs, beaten (or egg substitute equivalent to 2 eggs)
  ¼ c milk (regular or nonfat)

3–4 slices mozzarella cheese
Parmesan cheese (about ¼ cup)
16 oz of bottled spaghetti sauce, or the following:
  1 onion, chopped
  2 cloves garlic, minced
  2 T oil
  1 tsp oregano
  ½ tsp thyme
  ½ tsp parsley flakes
  ½ tsp salt
  dash of pepper
  1 can (15 oz) tomato sauce

Cook onions and garlic in oil until browned. Add other sauce ingredients, and simmer while spaghetti is cooking.

Preheat oven to 350°. Grease a large pie pan with some margarine. Cook and drain the spaghetti, rinsing with cold water. Also rinse cooking pan with cold water. Drain well. Put the spaghetti back in the pan and mix with the milk and eggs. Place the mixture in the pie pan and top with the tomato sauce and the cheeses. Bake for 25 to 30 minutes. Remove from oven and let it set at room temperature for 10 to 15 minutes before slicing. Slice like a pie, into triangles. Serves four.

TIJUANA CASSEROLE (MILK)

Serve this with real or Diet Sour Cream—the recipe follows. May be served with tortilla or corn chips.

  1 c cooked rice
  1 can (16 oz) whole-kernel corn (drained)
  1 can (15 oz) chili beans in sauce, or 2 c cooked pinto beans
    (if using home-cooked beans, add 1 tsp chili powder)
  1 can (8 oz) tomato sauce
  2 slices American cheese

Preheat oven to 350°. Spread rice in the bottom of a greased casserole. Cover with the corn and beans. Pour the tomato sauce over all. Top with the 2 cheese slices. Bake for 20 minutes, or until cheese melts. Serves four.

Diet "Sour Cream"

1 c nonfat or low-fat cottage cheese
3 T milk (skim or nonfat)
1 T lemon juice

Place all ingredients in a blender and blend for 2 minutes.

TOFU CHOP SUEY (PARVE)

For a delightful meal, start some rice cooking before you make the chop suey. Tofu looks something like cheese, but is made of soy beans.

2 T oil
1 10 oz pkg firm tofu
1 clove garlic, minced
1 small onion
4–5 mushrooms
3–4 leaves bok choi or Swiss chard
1 rib celery
½ cup bean sprouts
1 small zucchini, or stalk of broccoli
2 T chopped bell pepper
¼ tsp ground ginger
2 T low-sodium or regular soy sauce
1 T water

Cut tofu into cubes. Slice and dice the vegetables. Heat the oil in a wok or large frying pan over medium high heat. Cook the garlic and tofu in the oil for about 5 minutes, stirring. Add all the vegetables and heat them, stirring well. After 3 minutes, add the ginger, soy sauce, and water. Stir well for about 3 minutes more. The chop suey is done as soon as the vegetables are heated through. Serve with rice. Serves four.

VEGETARIAN CHILI (PARVE)

½ lb dried pinto beans
water
2 T oil
1 medium onion, chopped
1 clove garlic, minced
½ bell pepper, diced (or use frozen peppers)
1 tsp dried or 1 T chopped fresh parsley
1 can (6 oz) tomato paste
1 tsp chili powder (or to taste)
½ tsp cumin
dash pepper
1 tsp salt, or to taste

Wash beans and cover with water. Bring to a boil and boil for 5 minutes. Remove from heat, cover, and let stand 1 hour. Bring beans to a boil again, lower heat, and simmer for 30 minutes. Heat oil in another pan and brown onion, garlic, and bell pepper. Add to the beans along with other ingredients except salt. Simmer for 1 hour or more, until beans are tender. Add salt if desired. Serves six.

ZUCCHINI PARMESAN (MILK)

Anyone who has ever had a successful summer vegetable garden knows how wily zucchini can be—hiding under the leaves until they reach baseball-bat proportions. Even if you do not have such a garden, you may know someone who does and keeps giving you gifts of big zucchini. For those of us who do not have a garden or a friend who has one, there are still tempting supermarket specials.

2 T oil
1–2 cloves garlic, minced
1 large onion, diced
1 large or 3–4 regular sized zucchini
1 can (8 oz) tomato sauce
pepper and salt to taste
1 tsp oregano
6 oz sliced mozzarella cheese
¼ c grated Parmesan cheese

Preheat oven to 350°. Brown onion and garlic in the oil. Grease a
9 by 13 inch pan and place the onion and garlic in the pan. Slice the
zucchini and add to the onion and garlic. Top with the other ingredients and then place in the oven and cook, uncovered for 20 minutes. Cover pan with a cover or some foil and bake 20 minutes
longer, or until zucchini is tender. Serves four.

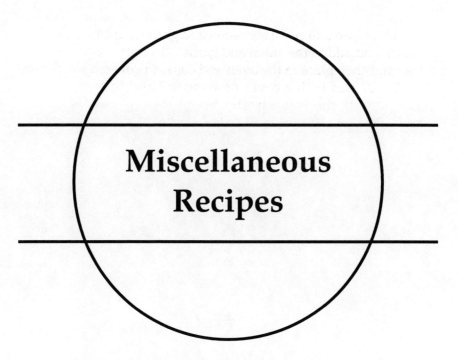

Miscellaneous Recipes

Here are some recipes that were too good to leave out but baffling as to where to include!

ALCOHOLIC PUNCH (PARVE)

A party favorite.

6 oz lemon juice (equivalent to ¾ c)
12 oz frozen orange juice concentrate
1 fifth (6 oz) vodka
1 qt club soda
1½ qt ginger ale
orange slices

Pour into a punch bowl and add a chunk of ice. Makes about forty servings.

LEMON MARMALADE (PARVE)

See the Pineapple Jam recipe for hints on the processing procedure.

6 lemons
1½ c bottled distilled water
⅛ tsp baking soda
5 c sugar
1 pouch liquid pectin

Peel lemons—but peel thinly, to avoid the white part of the peeling. Cut the rind into slivers and put in a large pot. Remove the white peeling from the lemons and discard. Section the lemons, remove the seeds, and cut the lemons up. Then set them aside. Measure the sugar and set aside. Combine the baking soda and water with the sliced rind. Heat to boiling and simmer for about 20 minutes, watching that the water does not boil away. Add sugar and lemon. Cook, stirring, until mixture reaches a full boil. Boil hard for 1 minute. Remove from heat and stir in the pectin. Skim any foam from the top. Let stand for 5 minutes, stirring occasionally. Pour into sterilized preserve jars, filling to ¼ inch of the top. Adjust the caps and then process for 10 minutes in a boiling water bath. Gently shake the bottles twice during cooling. Makes about 4 half pints.

PINEAPPLE JAM (PARVE)

They don't seem to sell pineapple jam in the stores anymore. A boiling water canner is required, and standard canning jars.

2 cans (20 oz each) crushed pineapple (undrained)
1 pkg pectin
5 c sugar

Sterilize 3 full-pint or 6 half-pint canning jars. Put the covers in hot water over a low heat. Measure out 4 cups pineapple and put in a large pot with the pectin. It is preferable to use an enamel pot. Bring to a boil and then stir in the sugar. Bring to a full boil and boil, stirring, for 4 minutes exactly. Remove from heat. Put the jam in the jars, leaving ¼ inch headroom at the top. Cover, following canning jar manufacturer's directions. Process underwater for 10 minutes in boiling water bath (the water must be really boiling for the whole 10 minutes). Remove the jars and let cool on a dish towel for several hours. Check to be sure the jar tops have developed a dent in the center and are properly sealed—if a jar has not sealed, the jam must be refrigerated and eaten. Otherwise, let the jars stand a week or so, to set, before using. Properly sterilized and sealed, jam keeps for months.

RICE STUFFING

I had a hard time finding leftover parve bread in our house in order to make bread stuffing, so I got into the habit of making a rice stuffing for turkey or chicken. It turned out to be a family favorite.

2 T oil or fat
1 small onion, diced
2 ribs celery, diced
2 c cooked rice
1 tsp parsley flakes or 1 T chopped fresh parsley
½ tsp poultry seasoning
salt and pepper to taste

Heat oil and brown onion and celery. Mix in other ingredients. Use to stuff poultry or breast of veal.

Glossary

Borscht A Russian-style soup made with beets or cabbage.

Challah Braided white bread, served on the Sabbath and holidays.

Chanukah The Festival of Lights, commemorating the rededication of the Holy Temple in Jerusalem.

Cholent A Sabbath food prepared on Friday and kept warm, to be served on Saturday.

Farfel Dried lumps of dough (similar to noodles) used in soups or puddings.

Gefilte fish A stuffed fish. It is cooked and chopped, and may be served hot or cold.

Gribnes Cracklings from rendered chicken fat.

Hamantaschen Triangular cookies served on the Purim holiday. The triangular shape recalls the hat that Haman wore.

Haroseth or Charoses Mixture of apples and nuts eaten on Passover, to remind us of the mortar used with bricks during Egyptian slavery.

Kashruth The dietary laws.

Kishka Stuffed beef intestines.

Kosher "Fit to eat"; food prepared in accordance with the Jewish Dietary Laws.

Kugel A pudding.

Latkes Pancakes.

Lox Smoked salmon.

Matzo Unleavened bread eaten during the eight days of Passover.

Mitzvah Literally a commandment, but also understood as a good deed.

Nosh   A snack, or to snack.

Parve   A neutral food that contains neither milk nor meat—such as fruit or vegetables.

Passover (Pesach)   The holiday commemorating the story, in the biblical Book of Exodus, of the freeing of the Israelites from Egyptian slavery.

Purim   The Feast of Lots, the holiday commemorating the story in the biblical Book of Esther.

Rosh Hashanah   The Jewish New Year.

Schmaltz   Rendered chicken or turkey fat.

Seder   The traditional Passover service and meal.

Shabbat   The day of rest, or Sabbath, begins at sunset on Friday and ends at sunset on Saturday.

Shavuoth   The Feast of Weeks (also known by the Greek name, Pentecost), celebrating the harvesting of the first fruits and the receiving of the Ten Commandments.

Shofar   A ram's horn, sounded on Rosh Hashanah and Yom Kippur.

Strudel   A pastry.

Sukkah   A hut constructed to celebrate the Sukkot festival. It is used for picnic meals and sometimes to sleep in.

Sukkot   The Feast of Tabernacles. It is a time of thanksgiving for the harvest and is also associated with the forty years that the Israelites wandered in the wilderness.

Torah   The Five Books of Moses; the Law; the Holy Scriptures; the Bible.

Tu B'Shevat   The New Year of the Trees. A special day to appreciate nature, to eat fruit, and to plant trees.

Tzimmes   A vegetable dish, usually containing carrots. It is a Yiddish word, which also means to make a fuss.

Yom Kippur   The Day of Atonement, a solemn fast day of reflection and prayer.

Index

ABOUT THE AUTHOR

Rosalyn F. Manesse is a registered nurse. She has years of experience as a religious school teacher and has been a newsletter editor and publicity chairperson. She is the author of thirty published magazine articles. Rosalyn and her husband, artist Ira Manesse, have three children and three grandchildren. They live in Southern California. This book is the product of thirty-six years of cooking.